THE SHUT-DOWN LEARNER

The Shut-Down Learner
Helping Your Academically Discouraged Child

RICHARD SELZNICK, PhD

Illustrations by Neil King

SENTIENT PUBLICATIONS

First Sentient Publications edition 2009
Copyright © 2009 by Richard Selznick, PhD

For permissions, see page 161.

A paperback original
Cover design by Kim Johansen, Black Dog Design
Book design by Timm Bryson

Library of Congress Cataloging-in-Publication Data
Selznick, Richard.
    The shut-down learner : helping your academically discouraged child /
Richard Selznick ; Illustrations by Neil King.
        p. cm.
ISBN 978-1-59181-078-0
    1. Slow learning children--Education--United States. 2. Learning disabled
children--Education--United States. I. Title.
LC4691.S45 2008
371.94--dc22
                                2008037620
Printed in the United States of America
10 9 8 7 6 5 4 3

SENTIENT PUBLICATIONS
A Limited Liability Company
1113 Spruce Street
Boulder, CO 80302
www.sentientpublications.com

*This book is dedicated to the memory
of my father, Mel Selznick, who would
never let a child shut down on his watch.*

*Reminding me that it "is often the intangibles
that matter most with children," no one understood
the art of developing a child's self-esteem better than he did.*

CONTENTS

What to Do with the Shut-Down Learner   57

The Shut-Down Learner's Perspective   115

Shut-Down Learner Success Stories   133

ACKNOWLEDGMENTS

This book was a long time in the making. Along the way so many people offered support, friendship, and advice. The following people contributed to the development of *The Shut-Down Learner* in their own way: Dr. John Kellmayer, Lisa Zeidner, Dr. Andrea Fina, Dr. William Sharrar, Dr. Michael Gallaway, Dr. Alan Schwartz, Robert Bodzin, Ben Yudin, Scott Silber, Dr. Stuart Chavis, Susan Chavis, Dr. Alan Mushnick, Gail Capaldi, Stephen Jackel, Robert Gross, Dr. Len Horowitz, Lis Weiss, Magge McCann, Steven Kessler, Susan Schulman, Marc Rosenthal, Dr. Leonard Krivy, Dr. Joan Krivy, Michael Gaier, Kevin DiPietropolo, Michael Segal, Tim Murtha, Mare Rivera, Susan Buzzard, Alex Albrecht, Helen Pearson, Bill Albrecht, Andrea Hernberg, Josh Hernberg, Kendal Ellis, Donnie Chambers, Daniel Mitchell, Alyssa Marsdale, Danny O'Malley, the Cooper Learning Center staff, the faculty and staff of the Pediatric Department of Cooper University Hospital, and all of the parents and kids I've seen over the years.

Connie Shaw of Sentient Publications has been a wonderful editor and quarterback for the project.

I would like to thank my agent, Jodie Rhodes of Jodie Rhodes Literary Agency, for believing in *The Shut-Down Learner* and for her hard work in finding a good home for the book.

Lori Joyce, Assistant Professor of Communications at Gloucester County College, was extremely helpful as an editor. She was instrumental in helping move the book to its final stages.

Thank you to Neil King (www.boldfacedcomics.com) for bringing his artistic expertise to *The Shut-Down Learner.*

As a mentor and friend, Renee Evenson (www.bullseyepublishing.com) freely shared her wisdom and experience. I am very appreciative of all that she has offered.

A special thanks to Patrick ("The Photographer") Flanigan, for all of his effort, friendship, and complete belief in *The Shut-Down Learner.* Meeting at the "office" was thoroughly enjoyable.

Lloyd Stone (www.mannystone.com), my dear friend from the old neighborhood, was invaluable as a sounding board. As a self-admitted SDL, Lloyd's perspective and friendship were always valued.

My children, Julia and Daniel, kept me humble and laughing at myself. They always help to remind me what matters in life.

I am indebted to my beautiful wife, Gail, for all of her wisdom, love, and patience. She continually grounds me — never an easy feat.

The memory of my parents, Mel and Betty, and my grandparents, Eva, Sol, John, and Flo, is infused in the book and everything that I try to accomplish.

FOREWORD:
A PEDIATRICIAN'S PERSPECTIVE

I have been a practicing general pediatrician for more than thirty years and in the course of that time have gained some understanding of children. Every child is diffcrent. Every child has his own personality, temperament, strength, and cultural background. I know that children love to learn and look forward to different learning experiences. When things are going well, they love to go to school. If a child in kindergarten or first grade is not enjoying school, this is a problem that needs further investigation immediately.

The work of childhood is navigating the waters of school. For many reasons, not all children do well in school. When children struggle in school, their whole family system is affected. From my perspective as a pediatrician, the child's health is affected by her negative school experiences. Increased incidents of depression, anxiety, and family turmoil are the common side-effects of school struggling. By the time the child is in her teens, it is often too late to break the downward spiral.

Learning occurs best when a child has a good night's sleep, a full belly, and a stable home life. But even with these advantages, some children have difficulty in the traditional classroom and experience school failure. Many of these children are bright and creative but their strengths remain unrecognized and unrewarded. *The Shut-Down Learner* speaks well to these issues.

There is a wide variation in biological talents and predispositions. Some of us show abilities in math and science, others in music, literature, and the arts. Many people in society are wonderful visual thinkers, while others are more verbally oriented. Our society is built upon these differences. We need our artists, engineers, scientists, teachers, scholars, and our everyday workers. Yet, so many people are discouraged because they are casualties of their school experiences.

Parents are greatly stressed when their children are having school difficulty. School failure is viewed as an ominous sign of future failure. Parents become rightfully anxious as to what will happen to their children if the downward spiral continues.

It is important for parents with such children to read *The Shut-Down Learner* to get a better perspective on what their child is facing. Shut-down learners come in a variety of shapes and sizes. Labels do not describe them very well. (Actually, labels do not describe children well, in general.) Dr. Selznick states that one of the most significant variables that these children share is their talent in the visual-spatial dimension of their ability, coupled with their dislike and discomfort with reading, spelling, and writing. What they also share is a series of failures leading to frustration, lowered self-esteem and, often, anger.

I agree with Dr. Selznick. I do not believe that children are lazy or difficult or just unmotivated. The shut-down learner has been defeated by the system and by misunderstanding. These children care a great deal about their learning and are looking to adults for help and encouragement. Dr. Selznick makes a strong argument that all struggling children should be evaluated with an emphasis on their strengths. He notes that the most important thing you can do for a shut-down learner is to help him accept himself and his abilities and to overcome his negative self-perception. It is important that parents understand this.

Dr. Selznick not only challenges parents to gain a better understanding of their children, but also challenges the schools to understand how these children shut down. Wholesale revamping of curriculum is not being suggested, and small changes can be easily accomplished. Children can be mentored. They can be encouraged. Teachers play a central role in altering the child's negative belief patterns. The key is relationship building. This does not cost money. It takes time. As Dr. Selznick points out, sometimes taking a child for a walk or sharing a soda will long be remembered. Just conveying to the child that he is valued is enormously important on so many levels.

It is important that the primary care physician, the parents, and the teachers understand the shut-down learner child described in this book so these children do feel valued and do not, ultimately, shut down.

William G. Sharrar, MD
CHIEF OF PEDIATRICS
Cooper University Hospital and
The Children's Regional Hospital

PROFESSOR OF PEDIATRICS
UMDNJ-Robert Wood Johnson Medical School

PREFACE

Why This Book Was Written

The primary purpose of *The Shut-Down Learner* is to give the parent of a struggling child perspective and hope. Practically every day of my professional career, parents come to my office worried about their children. Whether the child is in first grade, middle school, high school, or college, the concerns echo the same themes: Can my child handle the demands being placed on him? Are there identifiable issues that explain why he is struggling? How can we keep him from not becoming overly discouraged? How can we overcome his sense of discouragement and give him a sense of self-worth?

I have strived to present information to parents in straightforward, down-to-earth terms to put them at ease and to offer them a perspective that appreciates their child's strengths. Too often, these strengths are overlooked among the weaknesses that are magnified by the demands of the curriculum and the child's great difficulty in meeting those demands.

I have met so many shut-down learners over the years. While they were in the middle of their anguish relative to school, things seemed hopeless indeed. So many of these shut-down learners have become productive adults, eventually following job paths where their strengths became realized. Many of them did not follow traditional academic paths.

Is This Book for You?

There are many fine books concerning children's struggles in school. Each has its own perspective on the factors and ultimate solutions for a child's academic problems. No book can answer all of the issues raised about a struggling child. *The Shut-Down Learner* cannot be all things to all people. However, this book is for you if your child is discouraged about school and you do not know where to turn or how to help your child. The book's emphasis on understanding and reducing the tension in the household around academic issues will not take a lot of resources. Once a child feels understood, she often has more emotional energy for difficult tasks and challenges.

It is important to understand that there is never "the solution" when it comes to addressing children and the complex issues they face. If you as a parent or educator take away a broader perspective along with a couple of ideas to help reduce the tension or to increase the child's sense of self-worth, then the goals of writing this book will have been met.

THE SHUT-DOWN LEARNER

The Shut-Down
Learner Introduced

Spiraling Down

Nicholas was unhappy. He came to my office with his parents. They wanted to discuss his school problems. In tenth grade, Nicholas was in serious danger of failing almost all of his subjects. He told his parents he wanted to quit school and get a job.

His hat was pulled down over his forehead, keeping his eyes in a shadow. "He's ADHD [attention deficit hyperactivity disordered]," said his mother. "He's been on medication since he was in first grade. The problem is he keeps failing and spiraling down. We don't know what to do."

"What have you done to date?" I asked.

"Well, we've seen a number of doctors over the years. They just keep telling us he's attention deficit hyperactivity disordered. They either increase his dose of medication or change the dosage. There must be something else going on with him."

Sullen and Miserable

Darkness emanated from Nicholas. He was sick of doctors. He'd had it with attention deficit hyperactivity disorder, a story he'd heard many times. He did not believe that he had ADHD. No one had explained it to him in a way that he understood. He refused to take his medication. "They're not going to keep drugging me," he told his mother.

If he had ADHD, there was much more to it than the interventions that had been tried to date had addressed. There was more to the story.

His is the story of the shut-down learner. There are no easy solutions or simple formulas. However, if this child is understood and supported, this shut-down style can be averted. Years of anguish, frustration, and tension in the household can be greatly reduced.

What was most evident in talking to Nicholas was that he had totally shut down from the accumulated years of negative school experiences. He typifies the child who is the focus of this book — the shut-down learner.

The first step and possibly the largest step toward helping the child is to understand him and determine what has led to his being shut down.

Oversimplified Label

The diagnosis or label of ADHD (sometimes referred to as ADD) has oversimplified Nicholas. This problem of oversimplification became clear once I started working with him. Many other variables were at work that this label didn't explain. This book will explore these variables and scenarios that contribute to the child shutting down. Additionally, it will offer specific solutions and concrete approaches to implement that will help point the way in turning around this slide into becoming shut down.

The shut-down learner (SDL) represents a certain type of child I have seen countless times for an evaluation and consultation with parents.

At best these students are a challenge. They challenge parents, schools, psychologists, counselors, physicians, and any other professional trying to "fix" them. Often these kids are flat-out impossible to manage. They are resistant to interventions. They see nothing wrong and usually want to be left alone.

Overcoming the Shame: Getting to the Other Side

Shut-down learners come in a variety of different shapes and sizes. They are not all miserable and sullen, like Nicholas, but even if they are socially pleasant, they all share an underlying frustration with school. This frustration has led to embarrassment and shame along the way. Often this is acutely felt; sometimes it is experienced as a low-level underlying emotion. Even if it seems like he is coping, the typical shut-down learner becomes increasingly insecure as he proceeds through the grades.

There are common themes with most shut-down learners, even if personality variables result in different styles. I know many very successful adults who are former shut-down learners. They come from a variety of different fields and professions. These professionals include high-level executives, CEOs of companies, engineers, photographers, graphic designers, exhibit designers and producers, surgeons, landscapers, musicians, and trades people. The most significant variable they share is their talent in the visual-spatial dimension of ability (explained in depth later), coupled with their dislike and discomfort with reading, spelling, and writing.

Labels do not well describe shut-down learners. Some are called dyslexic, others learning disabled and attention deficit hyperactivity disordered. The label overly focuses on the deficit, on what he or she cannot do (such as read well, pay attention, learn effectively). The shut-down learners that I have known are incredibly talented and misunderstood. Sadly, many of them are casualties of school. Their self-esteem is so beaten down and their sense of shame and defectiveness runs so deep that they cannot overcome these emotions. However, there are those who make it to the other side and are enjoying very productive, satisfying lives. This book will explore the variables that enabled them to get to this successful other side, putting the shame and embarrassment experienced in school behind them.

Style I: Disconnected, Unmotivated, and Difficult

One of the more common SDL types and possibly the most challenging to manage are the ones such as Nicholas. I call this type Style I. In class they are bored and disconnected. They come across in almost all of their classes with a demeanor that says, "I don't give a sh-t." This sets in motion a vicious cycle between the child and the teacher. The child usually loses. While not all SDL types have this demeanor and personality style, a significant percentage do. They are the most difficult to deal with successfully. Typically, they are the male SDLs.

How did the child become this type of SDL? What set of circumstances led to this disconnected and sullen style? There are many factors that emerge from the early grades that accumulate and snowball negatively for the child.

Starting in the upper elementary school grades, these kids become increasingly disconnected, unmotivated, and difficult to manage. Why? There are cracks in the child's foundation that are largely unaddressed or unrecognized. Sometimes, like Nicholas, these cracks are treated entirely by medication. This approach does not address the skill deficits maintained by the child. In some ways, it serves to cover them up. As these skills are not addressed, the amount of work and the demands increase considerably. By middle school and early high school, they are almost totally shut down in relation to school. The Style I child feels trapped and smothered by the upper grades.

SHUT-DOWN LEARNER SIGNS

The following typically start to emerge in the upper elementary grades, becoming much more pronounced by high school:

- A sense that the child is increasingly disconnected, discouraged, and unmotivated (shut down)
- Fundamental skill weaknesses with reading, writing, and spelling, leading to lowered self-esteem
- Increased avoidance of school tasks such as homework
- Dislike of reading
- Hatred of writing
- Little to no gratification from school
- Increasing anger toward school

The crime of managing a shut-down learner such as Nicholas without understanding the larger picture and the numerous variables interacting with him is that much more could have been done with him. These kids desperately need to be understood. If the parents were advised earlier that there were other things to do besides focusing solely on medication, Nicholas may not be in the straits he is in at this point in his life.

This is not an anti-medication book. I am not suggesting that Nicholas did not need medication. In fact, he did. The major premise of this book is that this treatment was only one part of a much more complex profile that needed to be understood by everyone — Nicholas' parents, his teachers, and most of all himself. This approach takes a great deal of effort over a long period of time, but fully understanding the SDL truly benefits all interested parties.

I hope this book will help parents and professionals identify and understand these children more effectively. Once these children are better identified in terms of their strengths and weaknesses, natural recommendations emerge, with concrete interventions offered to help open them up to their own possibilities.

Style II: Pleasant and Terribly Insecure

Style II SDLs are harder to detect. Here's a typical teacher description of a Style II SDL whom I assessed recently:

> Sara, fifteen, is a pleasure to have in class. She always enters the class smiling and seems to get along very well with other kids. During class, though, Sara never participates, and it always seems as if her mind is elsewhere. Sara's work reflects a general lack of effort. It's almost as if she doesn't care.

My assessment of Sara revealed that there were many issues not being detected by the teacher. Specifically, Sara was poorly equipped to manage the long and dense reading selections that were typical of high school. A weak vocabulary, coupled with a lack of general knowledge, produced a poor ability to process what she read. Sara's active working memory also was quite weak. In contrast, Sara was well above average with tasks that were more visual in nature.

Sara's insecurity was also very evident. It was clear that she felt poorly equipped to manage her classes. Her demeanor in school was largely a cover-up designed to keep others from seeing how embarrassed and insecure she felt.

The Style II kids such as Sara have learned one thing that has served them well: they are good at navigating the social waters. Thus, teachers and other adults see them as positive and engaging. They are a clear contrast to the Style I SDL, like Nicholas.

Both Style I and Style II SDL kids share many characteristics. These will be described in detail in the next section. Their most significant shared trait is their inability to manage the major subjects in the standard curriculum in school. Both types are very insecure. Both find the demands of the standard curriculum are wearing them down, leaving them depleted and increasingly disconnected. In obvious and not-so-obvious ways, they are shutting down and becoming increasingly difficult to manage.

Whether of the Style I or Style II variety, all SDLs share the characteristics that are described in the following sections.

In the Beginning

Children enter school optimistically. They look forward to meeting their teacher and learning new things, such as how to read and spell. This optimism fades quickly for our future SDL. Rather than progressing at a normal pace, they find that acquiring these core skills becomes an enormous chore — a laborious, shameful process.

Can these children be easily distinguished in the preschool class? On the surface, no, they look like everyone else. There are often certain noticeable weaknesses, however, that are clues to the shut-down style that emerges in the upper grades. The clues can be found in difficulty with certain tasks.

Imagine you are a six-year-old child in a first-grade class. You are excited. This is the big league — first grade. This is when you'll get those amazing powers that adults have. You'll start reading.

What happens when these skills are not easily acquired? How will that make you feel? What if everyone around you seems to be getting it, but you don't?

You look around the room. Many of your friends are reading out loud already. You wonder quietly to yourself, "How did they learn *that?*"

To understand how this feels, put yourself in this situation. Imagine there is a group of children who meet a teacher at a track every morning with their bicycles. Each time the teacher says to the children, "Okay everyone, time to get on your bikes." There is an assumption that all of the kids will be able to get on and ride at the teacher's command. About seven out of ten kids hop readily on their bikes and start riding. Three or so look embarrassed, staring sheepishly at the ground. They can't ride well. You are one of the three. You remember how it felt yesterday when you couldn't get on the bike with the others. You feel defeated, and it's awful. Now the teacher is asking you to do it again. You know how much it hurts to fall — to fail.

You give it a try because you remember what your parents said before you went to the track today after you sobbed that you did not want to go back. They said, "All we want you to do is try your best."

Didn't they know that you did try very hard yesterday? It didn't matter. You still couldn't get on the bike. You wobbled and fell off almost immediately. Many of the other kids snickered at you as they rode around in circles. It felt horrible. You didn't want to face that again. Yet, every day you knew it was going to be the same.

This scenario is the same experience for a child who struggles in the early grades. The embarrassment and exposure are deeply felt, even if they are not shown. The reading lesson begins and every day it's the same, "Okay class, open your books." You look around while others start to read, and you begin faking it.

Early Red Flags

Lack of key skills contributes to difficulty with early reading. One such skill is the ability to rapidly identify and name letters. Children who are slow in developing this skill typically have trouble with early reading development.

Similarly, many of these kids have difficulty with tasks involving phonemic awareness. Phonemic awareness tasks involve the ability to manipulate and play with sounds (for example, "Say 'flat.' Now say it without saying the 'f' sound.") Phonemic awareness has been shown in research to be a powerful predictor of a child's ability to develop early reading, spelling, and writing skills. The weaknesses involved with blending and segmenting sounds are strong correlates to early reading difficulties.

Another red-flag indicator is how the child looks during circle time. Many of our future SDLs look like they are not following the songs or the discussions that are usually conducted in this type of activity. Typically it is thought that their inability to follow is a sign of ADHD. More often, I find the children have difficulty with the language demands of a typical circle-time activity. This difficulty with language processing is an important red-flag indicator.

These red flags or cracks in the foundation often are not readily apparent. In fact, these traits often remain overlooked. However, they are there in our future shut-down learners. Often these weaknesses are ascribed to other variables such as motivation ("He should try harder") or to ADHD ("He has a deficiency of attention"). These red flags will lead to later difficulty with phonics skills (decoding) and reading fluency. Without efficient and rapid letter-naming ability, phonemic awareness, and language processing, reading development typically occurs at a very slow, inefficient rate. This is the beginning of the descent into becoming a shut-down learner.

Younger SDL children witness their peers succeeding while they do not. Their parents become tense, frustrated, and frantic, which is conveyed to the child. Insecurity takes hold as the child experiences early failure. The child starts doubting himself deeply. This doubt becomes ingrained. Dejection and defeat replaces the once optimistic self.

CRACKS IN THE FOUNDATION:
PRESCHOOL, KINDERGARTEN, FIRST GRADE

- Doesn't love circle time, inattentive, rolls around on the floor
- Resistant to tackling early reading tasks
- Often slow with letter naming (or at least rapid letter naming)
- Not attuned to sound variation (be aware of chronic ear infections)
- Weak with phonemic-awareness activities
- Might not like being read to or listening to stories
- Might be overwhelmed by songs

The early seeds of insecurity are planted. The quiet sense of doubt and shame affects the child deeply, very early in her school career. These feelings become so well rooted that for many, they become impossible to overcome.

This debilitating cycle of early struggling, insecurity, and shame is the beginning of the educational career of the SDL. And it's not a strong start.

The Case of Catherine

Catherine, age five, is a spirited and spunky child. In her preschool class she is quite popular with everyone. In the class you can see her building, putting puzzles together, and making pictures. The teachers love Catherine, and she tends to get high praise for her involvement in class and her relationships with peers and adults. Most of her teachers would be surprised if Catherine one day became a shut-down learner who was discouraged and disconnected in school.

At home, though, Catherine's mother, Mrs. Finch, was worried. Mrs. Finch did all of the things that the preschool teachers suggested. Every night she read stories to Catherine. They played letter games, such as letter bingo and letter Go Fish. They made letters with finger paints and clay. Mrs. Finch tried everything she could to make learning fun.

Yet, it didn't seem to stick. Surely Catherine was learning some of the letters, but it seemed to be awfully slow going. Not wanting to compare, Mrs. Finch couldn't help reflect how much easier learning letters had been for Catherine's older sister. Even though the teachers kept telling her that her worries were groundless, Mrs. Finch couldn't stop herself. In her heart she knew there was something wrong. She wanted Catherine tested.

On the day of the testing, Catherine bounded into my office for her appointment. She connected with me easily. There were no signs of nervousness or anxiety. When it was time for her mother to step into the other room while I did my assessment, Catherine showed no sign of hesitancy.

The results were very interesting. Catherine loved doing all of the spatial and hands-on activities such as making puzzles, building block designs, and drawing pictures. In contrast, when it came to doing more of the letter- and language-related activities, she became much more fidgety and restless. There was a clear shift in her demeanor and confidence. I had to help her to stay on task and not give up readily, which she would do with these language-based activities.

One of the tests I gave Catherine was Early Reading Success Indicators. As her mom had suggested, Catherine was very weak with core tasks related to early development in reading. Catherine was quite weak on a rapid letter-naming task in which she was asked to read letters in a random order from a larger array. She also was very inefficient when rapidly naming objects and pictures in an array.

Finally, she had great confusion with the phonemic-awareness activities. These results suggested that Catherine was at some degree of risk for slow development in acquiring early reading skills.

These weaknesses were the early signs of Catherine becoming a later shut-down learner. As Catherine would come to find reading difficult, she would avoid it more and become resistant to school activities. In class, Catherine would be viewed as restless, distractible, and fidgety. The once happy and optimistic child in preschool would not be visible. Insecurity would dominate most of Catherine's academic activities. By third grade she would start to doubt herself, and by the upper elementary grades she would become increasingly avoidant of basic school expectations.

**GOOD ASSESSMENT ESSENTIALS:
DESCRIBING BEATS LABELING**

We are very often focused in schools and in the medical and psychological community on the diagnosis. Here are some tips on assessment:

- A good assessment is descriptive; you should come away with a solid understanding of your child's strengths as well his weaknesses.

- It is far better to find a professional who can help describe your child's strengths and weaknesses rather than determine a label to put on the child.

- Saying a child needs help with defining words but is better with spatial and visual tasks is much more helpful than simply saying the child is LD (learning disabled) or ADHD; such a statement focuses on the skill that needs development.

Fundamental Problems with
Reading, Spelling, and Writing

Research and clinical experience highlight this sorry fact — children unable to read and spell adequately in third grade are destined to a similar fate in middle school and high school years. The percentage of children expected to struggle in reading, spelling, and writing hovers around 30 percent in suburban schools, with the numbers soaring in poorer communities.

Almost all SDLs had early school problems in the fundamental skill areas of reading, spelling, and writing. Despite attempts from special educators and other remedial teachers to help the children avoid failure, the progress often is extremely slow, often unrecognizable. The specific aspects of the academic problems will be described later.

"He Can Do It If He Tries"

Even in this day and age, poor motivation too often is seen as the number one contributor to the child's problems. I continue to be amazed by the refrain, "He can do it if he tries," suggesting the child's problem is purely laziness. When I hear this from parents and teachers, I find myself thinking, "No he can't."

More often than not, laziness and low motivation are not the main culprits — they are the by-products of years of frustration.

Take Garrett, for example. Garrett, an eighth grader, is declining by degrees relative to school. Like air slowly going out of a tire, Garrett's motivation for school is diminishing. Garrett's father yells at him a great deal. His belief is that Garrett's lazy, which is the usual explanation.

> **COMMON PARENTAL INTERPRETATIONS**
>
> Parents will offer theories for why their child is shutting down in school. These are the more frequent:
> - He's lazy.
> - He just doesn't try enough.
> - He doesn't care.
> - He's not performing out of spite.
> - He has some kind of a disability, such as ADHD or LD.

After evaluating Garrett, I don't believe this is the reason for his school decline. All indicators from the assessment point to a host of pervasive inefficiencies. He wasn't severely deficient in different areas tested, just inefficient.

How does inefficiency lead to the state Garrett was in when I met him?

Imagine you're required every day to run a two-mile race. In the back of your heel you notice a tiny pain, like a heel spur. It's not enough to keep you from running; in fact it's not even something that the doctors could detect, but you know it's there. At first, you tough out the pain. It's not a big deal, and you know you have to run the race.

Over time though, your motivation for running declines. Running becomes a laborious, irritating chore that you flat-out detest.

That's how school is for Garrett. Children, in general, have a hard enough time reading long, extended text. Let's say that an average assignment takes an hour to complete. If it takes the SDL approximately double the time for the reading, only to leave him struggling and confused with what he read, what would happen to his motivation over time?

He would shut down — become frustrated and not particularly motivated for repeating this task.

Garrett's mother explained, "Well, we punished him last week. We took away his video games, and now he seems to be trying harder. We know he can do it if he tries."

Yes, and if you offered the runner a $5,000 prize for running the race, his motivation would probably increase — at least it would for the short term. This does not mean a person can "do it if he tries." What it means is that a more intense and stimulating consequence (positive or negative) can help a person ratchet down and try harder. This newfound motivation is rarely sustained, however. The inefficiencies ("heel spurs") grind down the motivation over time, resulting in the shut-down profile.

Sometimes trying isn't enough. I hope that by the end of this book it will be clear that the motivation problems plaguing the SDL are secondary to other core issues. Contrary to much in life, with the SDL you *can* tell which came first, the learning problem or the lack of motivation.

TYPICAL PARENT INTERVENTIONS

Typical parent responses center on certain erroneous beliefs. These include:

- The child will become motivated by a lot of yelling.
- The child will become motivated by increased punishments and loss of privileges.
- Rewards will motivate.

These are short-term solutions that frequently backfire.

Not Just Boys

Even though many of the examples in this text are boys, keep in mind that girls can be SDL types as well. They tend to present differently and often do not have the complete package of the SDL. Typically their social skills are more finely tuned, so they do not frustrate teachers and parents as the boys do.

The girls are usually more in the Style II category described earlier. They are not as sullen or as angry, on average, but their academic issues are very real.

The Shut-Down
Learner Described

What do shut-down learners look like? Are there typical character-istics or traits that can help identify them? Definitively, yes.

Consistent Profiles and Red Flags

The SDLs' profiles are fairly consistent. Their attributes are not all negative by a long shot. Some of the characteristics are assets, repre-senting real strengths for the child. Other characteristics are liabili-ties. The goal is to identify and capitalize on the strengths.

Not every SDL will have every one of the following characteris-tics, which should not dissuade parents from thinking of their child as a potential SDL if most of the characteristics apply.

Also it is important to understand that the child becomes shut down over years of cumulative negative experience. If your child is still fairly young, he may be showing red flags but not be fully shut

down. Many of the characteristics described can begin to be identified as early as preschool.

The High-Spatial Child

A primary trait or characteristic the SDL possesses is excellent spatial and visual perceptual organization skills. This attribute is his most defining indicator, and it is the most important one to understand. While the trait defines the child's core strength, it also represents one of the major reasons he is shut down and provides answers about what to do with this child.

HIGH-SPATIAL VS. LANGUAGE-BASED CHARACTERISTICS

High-spatial
- Lego kid
- Loves puzzles
- Engages for hours with hands-on activities
- Likes taking things apart to see how they work
- Enjoys hooking things up, such as entertainment systems
- Good awareness of visual detail
- Excellent visual recall
- Does well with psychological assessment tasks that involve spatial analysis
- Enjoys doing tasks and is movement-based

Language-based
- Good understanding of words and word usage
- Takes in verbal information well
- Socially personable with good verbal communication skills
- Can attend to lecture readily
- Enjoys reading
- Enjoys writing
- Follows verbal instructions well

What is a high-spatial child? Why is it so important to understand this term?

SDLs readily perceive patterns. They can visualize things well. Most of their thought process is dominated by visualization, as opposed to thinking through language. To explain it, let's look at tasks involved in day-to-day living. While no task is purely dominated by one trait (ability) or another, a task can be analyzed for its load, or its primary emphasis. Some tasks have a visual-spatial load, while others are language loaded.

For example, when one is speaking in front of an audience or a classroom, the load is in the area of language and verbal communication. While visual skills play a certain part, such as in reading the reactions of the audience, they are secondary abilities for the success of the task.

There are many tasks in life where the opposite skill is emphasized. For example, I bought a wine rack that needed assembling. The directions were almost all through pictorial diagrams, with little written explanation as to how to put it together. The load was visual, not language-based. That's why I suffered for hours trying to figure out how to put it together!

The SDL would look at the whole picture of the wine rack and put it together flawlessly within a short time. Struggling through the directions in a step-by-step manner is not something he would do. These children become fully engaged in tasks that load on spatial awareness, spatial perception, and visual analysis.

When the SDLs are engaged in tasks that require spatial aptitude, they rarely exhibit distractibility, hyperactivity, or restlessness. These children can engage in hands-on tasks for hours. Not all children are fully engaged with tasks such as these. This ability is the most important clue of all. While strength with such abilities is clearly a good quality, there is a flip side when the child is trying to operate in a primarily verbal environment such as school.

In effect, these kids see things differently than people who load on the verbal side. There are patterns and relationships to discern and perceive that are largely overlooked by the verbal types. Take a simple item such as a washcloth. For many, it's just a piece of material. To the person who is visual and spatial, it is much more. There

are subtle intricacies (such as the weaving) that are often overlooked by those who are not strong with these abilities.

Lego Kids

I also refer to high-spatial kids as Lego kids. Lego play is the perfect medium for the child who is being described. The colorful pieces, the potentially intricate connections, and the visual imagination all interacting make a perfect vehicle for the strengths of the high-spatial child.

In the conference setting, one parent after another will tell me that their kid loved to play with Lego bricks when they were younger. Questioning the child's interest in Legos is a standard approach I take with parents after I've started working with a child. A typical dialogue goes like this:

"Did he play with Legos much as a kid?"

"I couldn't take them away from him. He still loves to go into the basement and build with them. When he was five, he built these really complex designs from his mind. He was so creative. I thought he was a genius. What happened? How could he go from doing something so well to failing in school?"

What happened is the curriculum got in the way. The child was thriving when he was in a classroom that tapped into his strengths. As the curriculum shifted in the first grade to more language-based activities, the decline in confidence and performance started.

Beyond preschool and kindergarten, the environment and activities the child engages in change dramatically. The child goes from a very hands-on and visual world to one in which such activities are greatly reduced.

Thriving with Visual Tasks

It is a fundamental truth of human nature, not just in childhood, that we spend more time doing things we do well while avoiding the things we do poorly.

These children thrive when the load is more visual and spatial. All of a sudden their poor attention span and distractibility diminishes to the point of nonexistence. They are thoroughly enjoying these tasks and become fully engaged with them.

This phenomenon is what is so puzzling to the parents of children considered ADHD. Time and again the parents will ask, "Why can he play Legos for hours but not pay attention in school?"

They pay attention because they are in charge. They are in command. They are confident and successful. The tasks engage them and help them to keep their attention focused. They don't need medication one bit while playing these games, building, or put-

ting electronic projects together. Their attention system works fine when they are doing these activities.

Hooking Up the Electronic Systems

As the children get older, the high-spatial children show these visual-spatial traits in many different arenas. These kids are the ones everyone looks to for hooking up all of the wires and connections for the TV and the electronic systems. While the language types are scratching their heads reading the directions, the high-spatial kids already have the connections figured out. They can do these kinds of tasks with ease, while those of us who are more language loaded are just confused. There are some lucky people with language-based strengths who are also good with visual-spatial tasks, but I have found them to be in the minority.

Kids who are high-spatial tend to be taking things apart and putting them back together. They are usually very curious by nature, wanting to know how everything works. They have a strong capacity to determine the different assemblages within a system (anything mechanical, such as motors). They can sit for hours analyzing these things. These tasks fully engage their attention.

Loving Computers

High-spatial learners also are inclined to love computers for the same reasons. The computer medium is heavily loaded in the visual and spatial. These kids can spend hours on computers, not simply for the reasons typically ascribed (escape, entertainment). While those reasons are sometimes part of the story, a more significant reason is that the computer is their medium of strength. They are more comfortable spending time with computer-based tasks because they feel in control and confident, something they rarely feel in school.

Finding Clues in the Data

Clues about visual and spatial skills can be found in the psychological evaluations. The perceptual reasoning index of the Wechsler Intelligence Scale for Children IV is a good indicator of high spatial skills. Specific subtests such as Block Design and Matrix Reasoning are loaded for visual skills. These subtests include tasks involving visually perceiving connections and relationships. The SDL thrives on these tasks. He comes alive while matching blocks to spatial patterns. SDLs love it. High-spatial learners love it.

Let's look at Block Design. This task is one that most of the SDLs love. This exercise involves showing a child a visual-spatial pattern and having her match blocks to the pattern. The SDL participants' demeanor changes when doing this task. They go from dejection and frustration with the reading and language tasks to happiness, confidence, and cheerfulness.

Block Design

Another example is Matrix Reasoning, a nonverbal task. The following figure is a good example of the task.

Matrix Reasoning

Here the child is asked to analyze a series of visual patterns to determine their relationship and which one would belong in the empty box. As the task advances, these patterns become more abstract and complex.

Their performances on these tasks support the parents' description that the children can focus for hours if it's a task they enjoy. Indeed, these children can do Block Design and Matrix Reasoning tasks all day with little distraction and a great deal of focus. *The success they experience is motivating and refreshing, something they are not used to in school.*

Hands-on/Movement-based

Another defining variable of many SDLs is that they thrive on movement and activity. They want to be where the action is, particularly where there's a lot of energy. Too often it is this energy that gets them into difficulty in the classroom. For them, the classroom is particularly deadening because of the variables discussed earlier, such as the overemphasis on language-loaded activities like writing and listening to lectures.

When we give SDLs the opportunity to actively involve their whole bodies, they become much more alive. Like Tom Sawyer or Huck Finn, you can't tie them down for long. They fight against the demands of learning, and flee from the constraints of typical school activities.

What Does He Gravitate To?

Clues about these movement-based variables are often found in checklists and questionnaires completed by the parents. How does the child spend his free time? Where does he gravitate to when not in school? The high-spatial/Lego kids (later SDLs) tend to love the outdoors. For many, skateboarding keeps them going. They tend to be a bit thrill-seeking, performing tricks on bicycles, pushing themselves beyond limits of parental comfort. They are often the ramp kids you see in parks. These kids spend countless hours perfecting certain moves on skateboards and bikes without any sign of particular distractibility.

The Great Outdoors

These kids also love other outdoor activities that combine their visual interests and strengths. I recently assessed Brian, a twelve-year-old boy who struggled in school. His teachers saw him as disconnected, uninterested, and unmotivated. Yet his mother said he spent much of his weekend at the nearby pond collecting animal and plant life for elaborate terrariums that he set up in his garage. The terrariums were incredibly sophisticated, showing creativity and a real depth of understanding, yet the same kid was getting a D in science.

How is it that this child who loved nature and biology could do so poorly in school that he got a D in science? Why did his passion and love of science disappear in school? Why couldn't he show any of his enthusiasm for science to his teachers, who had no idea how bright and alive he was in this area?

The answer to these questions will become clearer as we proceed.

Weak Language Skills

If the SDL receives high points on a continuum for the visual and spatial, he receives lower scores for language skills.

As a general rule, these children score in the 75th percentile or better on visual-spatial and hands-on tasks. By contrast, they perform at or below the 40th percentile on language-based activities.

This fact is essential to understand, as it is a core feature of the SDL. *It is devastating in school to have the combination of high spatial skills and weak language abilities. This is the heart of this book. It is this combination that is the central issue.*

What are these language-based skills? Language is a complex domain most of us take for granted because most of our language skills are fairly well-developed by the age of five. Most people have enough fundamental language skills to communicate. Let's look at some of the areas that are usually weak with SDLs.

DEADLY COMBINATION: HIGH SPATIAL AND LOW VERBAL

- School is heavily loaded on the verbal skills side of the continuum.
- There is a clashing of brain styles between the curriculum of school and the high spatial skills of the SDL.
- High spatial plus weak verbal skills equals shut-down learner.

Sparse Vocabularies

SDL language skills have a flavor of not being fully developed. Sometimes it's subtle. Vocabulary is a great place to see the weakness.

Vocabulary knowledge represents a fundamental skill needed for reading comprehension, broad literacy, written expression, and verbal expression.

When asked to define a word, the SDL tends to have difficulty offering a fully expressed answer. Certain attributes of the word may be provided, but the SDL has trouble providing more complete explanations.

For example, when asked to define the word "island," an SDL said it was a "place with palm trees." I responded, "Okay, that's not bad, but can you explain this further?" She just stared, unable to elaborate. In her mind she defined island just fine.

Now it wasn't a bad answer. Her response certainly gave a sense that she knew the word, but it wasn't complete. Her reply didn't define the word that well, and the lack of elaboration is classic for this type of child.

For the SDL, language production can be very sparse. There is a sense of incomplete communication.

Here is another example from an SDL case:

"What's a cat?" Answer: "It has four legs with fur." This needs to be elaborated on, because lots of animals have four legs and fur.

One of the clearest examples of this difficulty with expressive vocabulary: when a child has little understanding of how to explain the definition of the word, he repeats it, thinking he's defined it. Here's an example:

"What's a car?"

"It's a car."

"But what is a car?"

Shrugging, with some exasperation and annoyance, "It's a car!"

This weakness with vocabulary becomes especially important in the middle school years because this is when more involved comprehension and information processing become central. Without adequate vocabulary, comprehension suffers dramatically, and without comprehension, the child feels completely lost.

Weak Knowledge Base

Background knowledge and a base of factual information are also essential skills for school success and reading. We think of reading as a one-way process. Through our eyeballs, the words come into our brain in one direction. But this is not the case. Good reading is interactive.

Take this example. Child A sits down to read a story about Eskimos entitled "The Eskimos' Challenge." While he doesn't know a lot about Eskimos, there are certain images that come to mind before he starts to read. He pictures Alaska, igloos, snow, dog sledding, and seals. He's even seen some pictures of native Eskimo crafts. He doesn't know what the Eskimos' challenge is, but he's formulated images from the title of the story. This occurs in the mind of a good reader before he even starts reading the story. Active visualization will have taken place.

Child B knows little about Eskimos. She doesn't know where they live or what they do. No images come to mind. While she may be able to read the story and understand some of the elements, her lack of knowledge about Eskimos clearly puts her at a disadvantage because she does not have the framework on which to build connections and comprehension.

Which child will do a better job with the story? I will put my money on Child A.

Activating knowledge illustrates the interactive nature of the reading process.

SDLs have as much trouble with factual information as they have with vocabulary. Questions assessing factual information, such as "Who wrote Macbeth?" and "Who was president of the United States during World War II?" lead to blank stares or answers revealing these weaknesses. *The lack of prior knowledge leads to poor comprehension.* Without an adequate knowledge base, a child is at a decided disadvantage while reading. There are fewer mental compartments available to store information. If you've never heard of a particular topic or subject, it will take longer for you to understand the topic in comparison to someone who has at least a passing familiarity with the topic. This inability to efficiently take in information is weaker than the SDLs' counterparts who have solidly developed language skills. The children with better background knowledge will have an easier time interacting with the material.

Background knowledge is primarily developed through reading. The wider and more broadly one has read, the more information and vocabulary that has been encountered and acquired. Because SDLs are reading aversive, this avoidance starts a vicious cycle. The lack of reading exposure leads to greater difficulty with reading and understanding.

It is my impression that many of the kids considered ADD or ADHD have difficulty, albeit subtle, with the processing of *complex verbal and written language*. While they may look severely inattentive, often their inattention is largely a functional weakness from taking in too much language and information that they do not understand readily. Their circuits become overloaded and shut down.

I see it in my office when the child's parents and I are talking too much. The child starts to disconnect. There's too much language. He shuts down before our eyes.

Low RPMs

Recently I attended a school conference with one of my classic SDLs, Justin. The conference included Justin and his parents, as well as school personnel. The contrast between Justin with his friends and Justin in the classroom was striking. In the hallway with his friends, he was highly energetic. In the classroom and in small groups, you'd see his head down on the desk, and he'd look very disconnected — pained.

Our conference went as follows:

"Justin," I said, "you look out of it, like you're in agony."

Justin grunted something back at me.

"Part of the problem the teachers have with you is you look like your light bulb's too dim, there's never any spark. Or to put it another way, your RPMs are running too slow."

Justin identified with the light bulb and car imagery. It worked for him, giving him something to hold onto in later sessions. Using visual metaphors helps these kids. They need to see it to understand it. Justin could totally relate to the car imagery. It was his world.

In later sessions and interactions with Justin, I would talk to him about his RPMs and how he could turn his energy up in the classroom. Encouraging him to find ways of getting more actively involved helped him to connect better with the teachers. Getting him to stop slumping forward on his desk was a good first step. The teachers started to see him in a different light.

Floppy Rudders: Nothing's Steering the Boat

Increasingly, there is a great deal of attention in the field of education and psychology focusing on the role of "executive functioning" as the core of so many learning issues. Think of executive functions as the mechanisms of the brain that help to steer and guide a person. They are the rudder on the boat or the conductor of the orchestra. Weak executive functioning leads to problems with:

- initiating
- planning
- organizing
- sustaining effort
- self-monitoring

Executive functions are slow to mature and often do not fully develop into early adulthood. For some, these functions do not mature until they are well into their thirties.

Middle school and high school represent periods of schooling where there is increased demand for well-developed executive functions. Changing classes, adjusting to the expectations of each teacher, and keeping track of numerous subjects places a premium on these abilities. If you have a floppy rudder, you are bobbing around in the water with no direction and nothing steering you.

Tin Ear for Language

Dr. Martha Denckla, the renowned neurologist and director of the Developmental Cognitive Neurology Clinic at the Kennedy-Krieger Institute, has studied learning disabilities extensively and says kids like this have a "tin ear for language." What a great way of understanding the issue. In the same way that some people have a tin ear for music, SDLs are predisposed to weaknesses with the different language skills.

It doesn't mean they can't do a certain task. It just means they're not very good at it because of the different elements of language and language processing that they are simply not adept at managing effectively.

WEAK VERBAL SKILLS

SDLs have a tin ear for language. Language-related tasks are not their natural strength. Signs of weakness include:

- Poor vocabulary
- Weak fund of general knowledge
- Poor listening skills
- Overwhelmed by too much verbal input
- Shorter, less-developed responses to questions
- Weak reading comprehension

Poor Comprehension

The weak language skills overlap with processing information in reading, which will be discussed in greater detail in following sections. In brief, if reading is understanding language in written form, it stands to reason that if the language-processing skills are poor, the capacity to understand and process written information also will be poor. This weakness is one of the reasons SDLs have insufficient reading comprehension skills, both on standardized tests and in functional textbook reading.

There's simply too much information for them to manage, and this weakness puts the SDL at a decided disadvantage.

Type I vs. Type II Reading Problems

Along with high spatial skills and weak language skills, the SDL invariably has reading, spelling, and writing problems.

There are two essential types of reading problems, each of which require a different treatment modality. I refer to children as falling into one of two categories — Type I or Type II. The problems fall somewhere on a continuum, from mild to moderate to severe.

Type I Readers

The Type I reader has difficulty with *phonological decoding,* translating the letters or spelling patterns of a written word into speech patterns to identify the word and to gain access to its meaning; and *reading fluency,* reading quickly, accurately, and with good expression.

Children who struggle with phonological decoding show erratic, inefficient development in word identification, word decoding, and oral reading. Years of my clinical experience and a tremendous body of research highlight that phonological decoding is a cornerstone skill for adequacy in school. Acquiring this skill is a major goal in the early elementary grades.

Without adequate decoding or reading fluency skills, school becomes an enormous and laborious chore. When decoding skills are poor, everything bottlenecks for the child. He does not progress normally and cannot savor everyday school experiences.

A wealth of research highlights that children as young as four and five can be identified as at risk with weaknesses shown in phonemic awareness and early letter/sound identification. Phonemic awareness is a splinter skill of language. It refers to the ability to manipulate and use different sounds. For example, if you ask a child to say the word *clip,* but then say it again without the *k* sound, this is a classic phonemic awareness task. Children who

have trouble with this type of task typically have difficulty developing phonological decoding skills. The weakness in one (phonemic awareness) correlates with skill in the other domain (phonological decoding).

Type I kids do not respond to typical classroom instructional methods for developing reading, such as literature-based approaches. They need to have the skill of phonological decoding taught directly with multisensory, language-based approaches. Multisensory methods are structured approaches that work simultaneously on different senses, such as the visual, auditory, and tactile. The earlier this skill is taught, the greater the likelihood the students will develop adequate early reading skills.

When the child does not receive appropriate interventions, the problem snowballs and affects all aspects of her functioning. In addition, Type I readers almost always have significant spelling and writing problems.

Phonological decoding deficits account for the vast majority of children referred for special education. Often erroneously referred to as a reading problem, the issue is much more pervasive. It is not simply a reading problem. It is a reading, spelling, and writing problem, affecting everything in school. Each year the problem gets worse unless significant and sometimes drastic measures are implemented to address the deficiencies.

When these deficits are present, multisyllabic words are particularly challenging to handle. The Informal Name Test is a nonstandardized test I created to screen for these problems. I simply ask the child to read a list of names as quickly as possible. By fourth grade an adequate reader can read the list pretty quickly and efficiently. Certainly by the end of elementary school virtually all adequate "decoders" can zip through the list. However, SDLs usually get stuck. Often they can't read the words at all or read some of the words accurately but with great hesitancy.

For example, take the name "Darcy," which is on the list.

This was transcribed from a recent assessment of a thirteen-year-old (seventh grader) that I conducted. The child read the name in the following manner: "Uhh [pause a second or two], Darky [one more second], no, Darcy."

That's highly inefficient. Good readers read the word (name) instantaneously without thinking. Multisyllabic words are the biggest hang-ups for weak readers. These words start to appear by the fourth-grade level. Also at this level the text becomes longer and more involved. Reading becomes a laborious chore. Is it any wonder that the child becomes disconnected and shut down? Who among us would want to sustain such pain on a regular (daily) basis?

Some children learn to compensate through strategies such as memorizing words. Others can't because their problems are too great, and they become overwhelmed, discouraged, and shut down.

Decoding problems affect reading fluency. Reading fluency refers to the capacity to read smoothly, effortlessly, and with good expression. A person with a reading fluency problem reads text out loud in a strained manner. The text does not flow smoothly. This difficulty with fluency greatly reduces one's capacity to understand the material. SDLs are typically dysfluent in reading, except for the category of readers described in the next section.

Type II Readers

Type II readers are very different from the Type I decoding-poor children. Type II kids decode and read fairly fluently. There is none of the word-reading inefficiencies common to the first type. However, they are at a loss as to what they have read.

At its extreme, the Type II child doesn't understand the meaning and details of a given passage. Frequently other language problems are underlying, such as weak vocabulary. Ask these children questions about what they've read and they stare at you blankly. They miss the details and the subtlety of the text. Higher-order questions, such as inferential reasoning and drawing conclusions, are particularly problematic.

Like Type I readers, they should be taught direct strategies for becoming more actively involved with the text.

To address these problems, structured comprehension methods should be taught and practiced repeatedly. These children need to internalize an approach to reading comprehension. A method such as Lindamood-Bell's Visualizing and Verbalizing for Language Comprehension and Thinking (www.lindamoodbell.com) is an example of the type of approach needed for Type II kids. This method actively trains children to visualize and form pictures while they are reading. The technique involves the child in a much more active and multisensory manner.

Similar approaches need to be taught to develop study skills and note-taking. The more actively engaged the child is in the process,

TYPE I VS. TYPE II READERS

Type I	Type II
• Difficulty in single word decoding	• Fluent oral reading
• Laborious, inefficient, halting reading, dysfluent oral reading	• Adequate spelling
	• Pervasive comprehension deficits (particularly with memory involved)
• Poor phonemic awareness	
• Poor spelling and writing	• Mechanistic and thoughtless reading

the greater the likelihood for comprehension. The greater exposure a student has to these methods, the greater likelihood these skills will be internalized.

Written Output Problems

Shut-down learners find writing deadly. For them, writing is an agonizing process. Writing is one of the most complex activities that a student (or anyone for that matter) must perform. There are so many cognitive skills loading when writing, that SDL children are simply overwhelmed by the process.

Children are often asked to write from open-ended prompts such as "Write about your weekend," or "Describe a movie that you really like." The open-ended nature of the task leaves many children at a loss. They don't know how to start and become quickly overwhelmed.

Let's say the teacher asks the children to write about their weekend, a typical open-ended writing prompt. Kids who are not SDL style children can get started producing a fairly decent paragraph or two. For the SDL, their thought process upon getting such a request from the teacher is something like the following, spread over the time they are supposed to be performing the task:

"Oh, man...writing...I hate writing...What did I do over the weekend...I don't even know how to spell weekend...Oh, man, where do I start? I didn't do anything this weekend. What am I going to write about? Look at Meghan over there...I can't stand her. She's already handed in her paragraph and I haven't even started...I hate writing. It always looks like such junk when I am finished... The time's almost up and I've written four words and now the teacher is going to tell me I have to finish it during recess or take it home because I wasn't paying attention....I hate writing. I hate Meghan."

The SDL really has no idea how to get started or how to link thoughts together in a coherent paragraph. They will need much more direct, structured instruction over time to begin to understand sentences and paragraphs. Simply doing more of it each day without direct instruction will not result in much improvement, but it will further the frustration and sense of agony.

Daily Experience of Frustration and Failure

Type I and Type II reading problems represent significant variables in the life of the shut-down learner. Since kindergarten and first grade, these problems have been present.

Daily experiences of failure and frustration result in a cumulative effect, leading the child to become discouraged. With the right type of early intensive remediation, much of this can be averted.

Frustration Abounding: Family and Social Variables

These children are a great source of frustration to parents. Often sullen and irritable, particularly about school, they don't tend to be particularly compliant or willing participants in afterschool activities or with homework. As they get older, they also gravitate toward children who are similar to themselves. They mutually support each other's negative demeanors.

These manifestations can be very disconcerting to parents. They see their child's lifestyle as one that is spiraling downward. At some point, parents give up, exhausted by the seemingly endless battles.

Wrung Out and Depleted

A mother of a shut-down learner recently spoke to me about her experiences with her son. "I'm wrung out," she said. "I'm depleted. He zaps me of all my energy. Every day it's the same."

I have heard these comments from mothers time and again about this kind of child.

Because very few people have taken the time to explain the makeup of the SDL to the parents, they interpret their child purely as unmotivated, lazy, and difficult. Usually this results in a cycle of punishment, anger, and resistance.

Much of the household tone is dependent upon how dejected and disconnected the child feels. If the child has given up, pervasive avoidance and shirking of day-to-day responsibilities is the result.

Inevitable household battles follow, which doesn't improve the situation.

Family Predisposition

Almost always, the shut-down learner child has a parent who was a shut-down learner when he or she was younger.

When a family comes in for a consultation on their child, there is a lengthy discussion that focuses on the child's history. Some of the questions center on the parents' own educational experiences. What were they like in school? Did they struggle? A typical answer to these questions is the following: "Are you kidding? I was exactly like her. I was able to get past it and I'm doing pretty well now, but it wasn't easy. I never really liked reading. I still don't, but I do read what I have to for my work. I hate to see her struggle; it's so familiar to me."

Not Independent

These children have an incredibly difficult time functioning independently at home. Average homework and reading assignments are a monumental challenge for the SDL. The sheer size of the tasks immediately leads to the shut-down response. Parents can help set a more reasonable structure with smaller goals. This will increase the likelihood of the child having a degree of success. The SDLs cannot complete assignments without intense structure and supervision. However, when the parents give a considerable amount of supervision, the interaction frequently becomes a screaming match between the parent and child.

The parents require active coaching on how to communicate with and deal with their children. Negative and irritable patterns of communication play out into the home arena. Parents need to be

educated on the variables of the SDL. Knowledge of the situation takes the heat out of the system. The parents can then begin to see their kids in a more positive light.

The parents need to adopt an objective but supportive tone with the child. While emphasizing that homework can be very troublesome, the parents need to do what they can to break down the material so it is more manageable.

Difficult to Manage in School

SDLs also are personally difficult to deal with in school. Looking bored and disconnected in class was never a way to improve relationships with teachers. The children typically feel that the teacher does not like them, even though they don't know the reasons. They feel they have done nothing to the teacher.

I have tried to help SDLs become more aware of the signals they are sending out in the classroom.

This approach usually falls on deaf ears. From the SDL's perspective, they're not to blame; it's the teacher who is unfair. They

---

EFFECTIVE WAYS OF APPROACHING THE SDL

Defensive and angry communication can quickly result from typical interactions. Communication can be very strained in the house. This is unproductive and does not lead toward the desired end of basic cooperation. Strive toward the following in talking with your SDL:

- Watch reactive comments spoken very emotionally.

- Speak in more measured, objective tones.

- Use "here's the deal" as a phrase to describe the possible choices and consequences (such as "Here's the deal, you can either choose this or that, but here's the consequence").

- Stick to your statement of the consequences, don't be squishy.

---

continue to lock horns with the teacher even if they're not doing anything overt.

The Case of Kyle

Most of the SDLs I meet have been put on medication at some point in their educational careers. Some have been on it for years; others have tried it for a period of time, with varying results. A common observation is that the medication helped the child focus for a period of time, but that the issues reemerged after a while.

Take Kyle, for example.

Kyle is a shut-down learner diagnosed some time ago as having an attention deficit hyperactivity disorder. He was put on medication in fourth grade to address his declining academic functioning, and it was reportedly helpful.

Over time, however, Kyle's school problems increased and his resistance and low motivation crept back by degrees until he became a full-blown shut-down child. In tenth grade he was still taking medication, loosely managed by his family physician.

The cracks in Kyle's foundation due to other issues not fully explained with the diagnosis of ADHD were now fully apparent. Kyle was a poor writer, and his comprehension skills were weak, even though he could decode text material fairly well. Kyle was overwhelmed by the amount of information he was asked to deal with in eighth through tenth grade. It was simply too much for his brain.

A high-spatial child, Kyle couldn't cope with the demands placed on him. He detested school and started to miss classes more frequently. He did not turn in assignments or turned them in late.

His teachers began to dislike him more and more because of his low energy tone in the classroom. Even though Kyle was never outright disrespectful, the bored tone, the head on the desk, and the missed assignments took their toll on his relationships with his teachers, and their willingness to work with him declined. They became tired of him.

When I met Kyle it was clear that the simple "take the pill and call me in six months" treatment he was receiving was not in his best interest.

The family was at a complete loss about what to do with him. There was constant friction and tension in the house relative to Kyle's posture toward school.

The issue being raised was not that the medication was inappropriate for Kyle at the time it was prescribed. It may have helped him some. Chances are stimulants would help most people focus better. The issue is that by overemphasizing the ADHD (which is what the professionals did in the first few years) and treating his problems only through medical interventions (and those very minimally managed), a great deal was not being addressed or understood.

Kyle's parents accepted what they were told by the physician who put him on medication, and did not question this further. Essentially, the doctor stated that the reason Kyle had school problems was because he had ADHD. There's an implied assumption: take this medication and things will be okay. The parents accepted this approach.

Rarely are parents told that the issues are much more complex.

Kyle's issues were quite involved and not being addressed or understood. There were many reasons for this. Insurance companies require doctors to treat patients quickly, so the medical model was overly emphasized in a situation where broader-based understanding and interventions would have been more appropriate. And like most parents, Kyle's mother and father just accept what they're told by their doctors.

Kyle's problems were classic for an SDL. His academic difficulties were not sufficiently severe to warrant him being classified as learning disabled, in part because the special education assessment model at the time required a significant discrepancy between IQ and academic achievement. Because Kyle had an average verbal IQ (lower end of average, 30th percentile), the special education team did not find a significant enough discrepancy between his academic achievement and his intelligence. This approach is flawed in terms of identifying children at risk. Many children, such as Kyle, have great

---

HELPFUL ASSESSMENTS

A good psychological evaluation can be very enlightening. The assessment should include these features:

- Assess cognitive abilities
- Assess academic abilities
- Assess emotional/behavioral factors
- Avoid an overly rigid adherence to the discrepancy formula for identifying learning disabilities
- Use a descriptive approach rather than relying on diagnostic labels
- The parents and child should come out with a jargon-free understanding of the child's strengths and weaknesses.

difficulty yet are not seen as eligible for services. Effectively, they fall in a gray zone. While some states are changing this approach to classifying a child as learning disabled, the practice is still common.

Matthew

Matthew's case also highlights many of the issues facing the SDL.

Matthew was a fourteen-year-old ninth-grade student. He was brought in for an evaluation and consultation because his mother did not feel that he was trying hard enough in school.

Behavioral checklists completed by his teacher, Ms. Capaldi, noted that Matthew was angry, resentful, and argumentative. Here are the teacher's exact words describing Matthew:

> Matthew needs close supervision to get through his assignments and he appears to attend only if he is interested in the task at hand.

Matthew has tremendous difficulty staying focused when managing any text material that involves subject matter with which he cannot relate well. For most subject matter, particularly with textbook writing, Matthew tends to turn off and shut down. He becomes frustrated and reactive when asked to perform basic tasks.

Matthew likes to build things and is good visually and with his hands. He can make elaborate figures with very little material. For example, he can work for hours with scraps of paper and tape.

As indicated by Ms. Capaldi, Matthew was seen by a physician who diagnosed him as having an attention deficit hyperactivity disorder. This evaluation was completed after a 20-minute consultation. The evaluation did not involve an assessment of his cognitive or academic skills, nor did the assessment consider emotional variables.

The physician recommended that Matthew begin a regimen of stimulant medication. This was his sole recommendation. No other suggestions were offered.

The mother was somewhat troubled by this recommendation, and reluctant to start her child on medication without further information. This was the primary reason for seeking my services.

Matthew's assessment was very enlightening. To begin with, Matthew was asked to copy (with paper and pencil) a series of shapes and designs and organize them on the page. As one might predict, Matthew did beautifully with this task. He also performed well on a range of other tasks involving a number of different skills and abilities. Thus, when putting blocks together to match different patterns and puzzle pieces into known forms, he performed with confidence. He also analyzed an array of visual patterns quite effectively. All of his strengths clustered with the tasks that were more hands-on and visual in nature. Matthew's abilities in those tasks fell within the 80th to 90th percentile.

In stark contrast, Matthew's verbal skills were quite weak. His fund of general knowledge and spoken vocabulary showed real limitations. Information that should have been easily a part of his world (such as "How many states are there in the U.S.?") was not available to him or was inefficiently accessed. Matthew's verbal abilities fell within a low average range (15th to 25th percentiles).

Also of great significance was the difficulty he encountered on measures involving recall (processing) of spoken information. Examples of these tasks included his ability to manage mental arithmetic word problems that were given to him out loud and his recall of a series of digits. Matthew's abilities in these tasks clustered within the 15th percentile.

It should not be surprising that Matthew's reading comprehension skills also were quite weak. This was particularly apparent on lengthier passages in which there were greater amounts of information to process. He also was able to deal with only simple factual questions, and unable to respond to any of the comprehension questions that assessed higher-order reasoning and thinking. He could not make inferences.

Matthew read in a labored and dysfluent manner. His reading sounded choppy and dull. By the time he got to the end of the text, he was very disconnected from the reading. Large words embedded into the text were huge hurdles for him. The whole reading process was inefficient and strained.

Matthew's writing was extremely problematic. The following are writing samples taken at different ages, presented exactly as Matthew wrote them. The words in brackets are my additions to clarify some of the words. For "Movie Story," Matthew was asked to write about a movie that he liked. "Violin Story" is based on a card from the Thematic Apperception Test, which shows a boy looking at a violin.

Movie Story: Age 12   I sol [saw] a move. About a person how [who] braeks his leg. Kat [Can't] ride in the race. So his sister wants to race as his and she win. So she goes to the campingcip [championship]. They find out that it is a girl. After she wins the campingcip. And they don't want her to get the par is [prize]. She gets it enewey [anyway].

Violin Story: Age 14   There wants was a boy in the 70's how [who] wanted to learn how to play the volin. But his family is too poor to have a volin lesson. So one day after school he's walking do the street and see's a volin store and on the window it says reparse [repairs] and lessons so he goes in and askes how much do volin lessons cost. The man says $2.50 a hour so the boy ask is there any way that I would be able to work here if you give me a lesson. The man said come back tomoro and I will tell you so the boy came back the next day and the man said yes.

The boy was so exide [excited] that he ran home and told his parants. So that night the boy went back and asked what time do I start. The man said tomoro at 8:00 p.m. when you get off the man also said that you have to bring your volin with you and that the lessons will be a half hour long the boy did and he likked the lessons.

The major reason for highlighting this case is to emphasize the variables contributing to Matthew's state of being shut down. To treat him primarily and solely as ADHD overlooks a range of crucial variables. Medication was an important component in Matthew's treatment, but to stop there would have been a major mistake.

Matthew's significant strengths in the areas described, as well as the weaknesses, needed understanding. Further, the tension between Matthew and his family was becoming increasingly problematic. They needed to see him in an entirely different light. While medication may have helped him, much more was needed. His interventions will be elaborated upon in a later section.

Interestingly, Matthew also was a boy with a strong entrepreneurial spirit. Starting in ninth grade, Matthew made quite a lot of money managing his own landscaping business in his neighborhood. His can-do spirit is well suggested in the violin story. I am fully confident that Matthew will run his own business one day and do quite well despite his severe learning issues.

Emily, Age 15

Emily, a fifteen-year-old sophomore, is a star athlete, popular with her friends and teachers. Emily plays on a number of teams and her parents hope she will receive a scholarship for her athletic endeavors.

Her parents have suspected that she has a learning problem, yet no teacher has raised this issue. Her report cards typically include comments such as "Emily is a pleasure and very sweet."

In class, Emily does not display the usual behaviors of an SDL. You do not find her slumping on her desk, yawning at the teacher, or looking bored or disconnected. However, Emily's parents have seen the cracks in the foundation that were not apparent in school. As a result, they requested to have Emily privately tested.

Testing with Emily certainly highlighted that there were issues affecting Emily's school development. Emily was clearly comfortable and confident with the range of nonverbal tasks given to her. She was adept at managing the Block Design patterns and the various Matrix Reasoning designs. In contrast, Emily's reading comprehension was very poor. She was disconnected from the text and not able to understand a great deal of the concepts or the higher-order reasoning that was typical of her grade. Emily's word knowledge and her capacity to explain different verbal concepts were also fairly weak.

In my experience, this combination of high spatial reasoning with weak verbal and reading comprehension skills is as commonly found among girls as boys. However, the girls' engagement with sports and social activities has the effect of masking the weaknesses so they are minimized and not seen as overly significant. The girls, then, are often not referred for an assessment, and they continue receiving praise and positive feedback, even though their standardized tests and actual functioning reveals their basic weaknesses. They too would benefit from the methods outlined in subsequent sections.

Characteristics Summarized

These characteristics are the cluster of traits seen time and again with the SDL. When Lego kids are given visual and hands-on tasks, they thrive. The problem is that school becomes much more language-based beyond first grade. By degrees the air becomes thinner for them. Increasingly, they start to suffer because they can't handle the demands and expectations put upon them.

Reading, spelling, and writing activities result in their bulb becoming dimmer. While medication may help to a degree, conceptualizing SDLs purely as ADHD is a mistake. The underlying strengths and weaknesses need full understanding and attention.

THE ESSENTIAL MINDSET FOR ASSESSMENTS

- Parents always want to know "what's wrong."
- More importantly, make sure to find out "what's right" from the assessment.
- Good assessments are as oriented to what is working well for your child as much as what is not.
- The most important thing to do is to follow your child's strengths. This is the ticket, ultimately, in knowing what to do for your child.

What to Do with the
Shut-Down Learner

Understanding: The First Step

There are no easy answers for helping an SDL — no simple formulas, no simple solutions. But with an array of different strategies, the cycle of failure, discouragement, and disconnection can be greatly minimized. The shut-down learner does not have to become so shut down.

The first step, which is often the toughest, is to understand the makeup of the child and what makes him tick. Above all, it is crucial to remember that school tends to be a very deadening environment for this child. For all of the reasons described earlier, it is a place where he receives little to no gratification or sense of pride. This is not to blame the school. It's just a bad fit.

Are there ways to counter these effects that lead to the child being disconnected? The more the child feels understood, the less tension there will be around school. This doesn't mean you let the child off

the hook with school. It means you understand what a deadly combination the school curriculum is coupled with your child's brain.

Think back to Garrett, the child who probably heard every day that he was lazy and should put in more effort. At one point in the middle of assessing Garrett, I stopped and said, "You're not lazy; you've got a certain type of a learning problem."

I explained how he was a high-spatial/Lego kid and that reading and writing were brutally difficult for him. This freed him emotionally. It was the first time anyone had conveyed understanding of what he was experiencing.

This understanding is crucial for parents, as they are the ones dealing with the frustration every day. They also are usually the ones yelling at the child or criticizing him too often. Understanding the child and the shut-down variables lessens the tension and frustration.

This understanding takes the heat out of the interaction between the parent and child. It is this tension that feeds into the child's ter-

> **STEPS TO UNDERSTANDING YOUR CHILD**
> - Start with a good evaluation
> - Make sure the evaluator is clear about your child's strengths. Don't just dwell on the weaknesses.
> - Put the strengths in a context of your own understanding. How do the identified strengths apply in your day-to-day understanding of the child?
> - Find frequent opportunities to acknowledge your child's display of the strength. ("Wow, you did a great job helping to organize the basement.")
> - Keep reminding your child of his positive qualities. You are overcoming a great deal of negativity. However, do not engage in phony cheerleading. Kids will see through it.

ribly negative view of himself. By the eighth grade Garret's fundamental belief is that he is a lazy screw-up. He has given up largely because failure leads to further failure, and there is no one in his life to counter this view.

Parents are too quick to want to fix the problem. In many ways there is no fix. It is not a mechanical problem that can be fixed. Your child is not a car engine that can be rewired. A curative step would be for parents to pause and reflect on the situation. This understanding leads to change.

Parents must see their child in a different light or no intervention or treatment will work. They must shift from a perspective that sees their child as lazy and unmotivated to one that understands how he got where he is today. This is enormously relieving to the child. She starts to see herself in a different light too.

This understanding is a huge shift, one that is a lot easier said than done. We tend to look at a child in general terms, saying, "He's

smart enough, so he can do it if he just stops goofing off." Well, often he can't, as I've tried to illustrate.

It is human nature to avoid things we do poorly. We tend to avoid
tasks, jobs, and activities that expose us and make us feel incompe-
tent. This experience is the dynamic for these kids in school where
every day they are exposed. Every day they are faced with feelings
of failure.

Stop Banging a Square Peg in a Round Hole

The normal curriculum does not work for these children. Major
subjects such as social studies, science, language arts, and math leave
them depleted. Yet we persist with these, largely because the curriculum is the way it has always been.

As a result, by the end of their schooling, these children are worn
down, angry, and not well-educated. In effect, they are resistant or
immune to traditional education. School represents a dead match
between the demands of the school curriculum and the neurologi-
cal and personality makeup of the child.

To avoid becoming angry, depleted, frustrated members of society by the time they're sixteen years of age, SDLs typically need a
very different type of school experience.

The reality of their neurodevelopmental wiring (high spatial and
weaker verbal skills, coupled with reading, spelling, writing weaknesses) is such that the standard five subjects are deadening to them. They
can see little relevance or value whatsoever in the material presented to
them. Even if they can perceive the importance of the subject, the difficulty they face managing it leaves them turned off to the material.

Continually banging a square peg into a round hole does no one
any good. While most children question the relevance of certain

subject matter ("I hate history! It's so boring!"), the children who are *not* shut down typically get something from the learning process, even if it is just decent grades.

Good grades and praise help sustain average or better students. They see the grades leading to something, even if it's something far down the road. Delaying gratification is something they can accept.

Not so for the SDL. You can try to convince them that the history of Europe or the understanding of cloud formations or algebraic equations will make them more well-rounded. They won't buy it.

Recently a shut-down learner told me in counseling there was "no f-ing way" Shakespeare had any meaning or relevance to his world. As much as I love Shakespeare, I silently agreed with him. He couldn't understand the language of Hamlet. The language demands were too great. They were simply too much for his spatial brain to process.

Grades also don't motivate SDLs like parents hope they will. Parents and teachers tell their kids that getting good grades will lead to other doors opening for them down the road. Down the road is too far off and the rewards too intangible. School is the ultimate delayed gratification (get good grades in high school, which leads to college and later graduate school, so you can get a good job one day). Delayed gratification is not a well-developed shut-down learner trait.

Is there a way of changing the standard curriculum for these children? If we hold to the typical five subjects, then these must be offered in a way they can grasp. Subject matter would need to be presented much more visually and tangibly, with a lot less lecture.

The problem is we are not facing the fact that the SDL type is very deficient in basic, core skills. They are being sent out into society without the capacity to read adequately. Their writing is much worse than their peers, and chances are their calculation skills are poor, particularly with arithmetic word problems. If this is true, how can the standard curriculum benefit them?

True Remedial Education

Increasingly, schools are more focused on core curriculum. As noted above, the core curriculum in its normal delivery is troublesome to the SDL.

These kids need much more basic remedial education to become reasonably competent adults. This does not mean they should be given dumbed-down school experiences. However, the academics need to be much more remedial in nature, specifically addressing key areas of core reading, spelling, writing, and math skills. This should be their primary academic experience. Of course, there can be a sprinkling of subject matter coming from core subjects, but the focus would be on remediation.

The other part of their day should be hands-on, with courses allowing them to flourish and show their true capabilities. Alternative schools have more hands-on courses that motivate this type of child. Building, creating, taking things apart and putting them back together will keep them connected much more than sitting in seven excruciating classes a day of academics. Learning to create and use the strengths they possess would give them a sense that they could be valued.

As an example, take Tyler, a fifteen-year-old SDL. In the academic remediation he receives, the focus is on developing Tyler's capacity to write a basic paragraph with five sentences. Most of the year will be spent developing this basic skill without shifting too much to other skills. Using his strengths and recognizing his weak areas, he is being helped to visually map his ideas.

A tutor who works closely with him to develop his sense of paragraph and sentence structure can help him internalize the basics of the writing process. The remediation is also working on his basic reading skills by using multisensory methodologies to help him read more fluently, to bring him roughly within the sixth-grade range. The academic goals are modest.

How do multisensory approaches differ from more traditional methods? Within this format, teaching is conducted by engaging the child as fully as possible through simultaneous stimulation of the visual, auditory, and kinesthetic senses. The child listens, hears, and touches material. The multisensory methods tend to be highly structured, sequential methods, developing one skill at a time.

Tyler also developed reading fluency by completing exercises in a home-based fluency program through our center. This program, called Great Leaps (www.greatleaps.com), provides exercises for the child to practice a few nights a week. The child does repeated reading exercises to improve his reading fluency.

The important point is that the process is remedial without bombarding the student with too much subject matter or work that has little or no connection to his world.

In the afternoons Tyler works in a greenhouse, an environment he loves. The school has worked out ways of tying in his greenhouse work with other content areas, such as basic math and science. By learning to categorize plants, he develops an understanding of basic taxonomy and organization. By developing concepts of the greenhouse environment, he learns about ecosystems.

This is the perfect blend for the SDL. The academics are specifically targeting his weak areas while the hands-on botany and greenhouse

work offers a tangible set of skills and experiences directly relevant to him. No longer is he crawling despondently to school.

Previously gloomy, disconnected and shut down, Tyler is much lighter and optimistic because there is a better match between his school experience and his neurodevelopmental strengths and weaknesses. These positive experiences erode the negativity and self-hatred.

Most of the shut-down kids I've met thrive with an academic experience such as Tyler's. Some kids I know mentored with a carpenter, others in automotive settings.

Unfortunately, such a curriculum frequently translates to parents as old-fashioned vocational tech. Admittedly, it's hard to find schools that understand a program such as the one I'm describing. What I am talking about is allowing a child to have a curriculum that is much more suited to his own learning style.

One of my favorite shut-down kids, Michael, is now an air-conditioning repairman. He's now thirty-five years old with a family. I can remember him saying, "You know, Selznick, somebody has to fix all of those air conditioners. I think I'd be good at that." This was from a kid who detested the rigors of school. Michael did no homework and could barely contain himself in class.

It is crucial for parents and counselors to follow the child's lead. What Michael was telling me was he was a high-spatial kid who would do well with hands-on tasks. The problem was that Michael's parents were both professionals who had academic aspirations for him. It took a while to help them understand the best fit for their son.

In this day and age, there are many more activities suited to the visual and hands-on learner. However, these opportunities are often not given to these children. There is fear that such a curriculum will doom a child to a difficult, unsatisfying career path.

Recharging the Battery: Forging Emotional Connections

Besides focusing on academics, it is essential that a child's emotional needs be addressed. This focus on emotional needs can occur in different ways. It does not mean the child must be in counseling or therapy, although that might be part of a program.

Schools often have a hard time paying attention to the emotional landscape of the child. Pressures and demands placed on teachers and support staff simply leave little time to address these complex issues. Relationship and trust building take time, especially for SDLs. They already have developed layers of defense.

I have always found schools to be well-intended regarding the child's emotional development. They want to reach a child, and they know there's a lot that needs to be done. Because of the large number of children that school staff are responsible for, it's

extremely difficult for them to give every child the kind of attention required.

In a typical middle school day, the average teacher comes into contact with 80 to 120 children. Beyond the classroom, not much more is possible than a brief hello or word or two of encouragement when passing in the halls. This limited amount of contact is not enough to break the cycle, to cut into the pervasive negative feelings of failure and frustration.

Gabrielle was in my office recently talking about the disconnectedness she feels in school. She is frequently ridiculed and made fun of by other kids. What Gabrielle needs more than anything is for someone to check in on her and connect with her once in a while. She needs the support of an understanding adult. I spoke to her counselor at school, who was more than willing to come up with a plan for Gabrielle. We agreed that one of the younger female teachers in the school (who had Gabrielle in a previous year and who Gabrielle seemed to like) would check in with her at least on a weekly basis. The teacher would take Gabrielle out of class and go for a little walk with her around the school grounds. This proved to be enormously beneficial for Gabrielle. It wasn't formal counseling, but it did the trick in terms of Gabrielle connecting better in school.

When I taught special education classes, there were certain children who needed more connection than others. These kids were obviously shut down and dejected. They reacted like outcasts in the system. Their anger and frustration were brought into the classroom. Many teachers found them impossible, and indeed they were challenging.

If I didn't establish deeper emotional connections with the children, then anger and frustration were all I got from them. I had to go beyond the norm with these kids. Sometimes during lunch period I'd take one or two of them for a walk to buy a soda or a pretzel from the nearby store.

This attempt communicated something to them in a nonverbal way. And this interaction was not a difficult thing to do. Sometimes it's the small things that have big impact. I don't hear enough of this happening in school for SDLs.

This act of making a connection helps recharge the battery for these kids. In a sense it gives them an emotional boost. A teacher's interest communicates to them that somebody cares enough to take the time to encourage them. This attention also reminds them they are liked for who they are, something they rarely experience in school (and sometimes not at home either).

Often these kids do not like themselves. When someone spends time with them, walking, talking, listening to music, sharing a soda, it provides them with a much-needed emotional charge.

When the day is over, it may be the walk to the store they remember above all of the content they were taught in school that day.

Most of the SDLs I know go through their school day with little direct contact from the teacher in the way that I am describing. In fact, most of the contact they do receive is negative. They are the ones who continually frustrate the teacher by not turning in their work or behaving negatively in the classroom.

FORGING EMOTIONAL CONNECTIONS

The most important thing to do for an SDL is to help them accept themselves and to overcome their negative self-perceptions. Most SDLs are dejected, discouraged, and despondent. Teachers and parents can play an enormous role in helping the SDL become connected.

It is so essential that your child starts to feel good about himself.

- Convey to the child that he is okay. Enjoy the SDL for his many gifts.
- Watch critical tone. Don't put the child on the defensive.
- Admire small successes. ("Wow, look at you.")
- Celebrate frequently. Go out for a treat or something similar when child has done something well relative to school. Do not get into large monetary rewards.
- Help the child to see that the future is not hopeless. She must see that there are possibilities.
- Be encouraging!

Is there a teacher your child feels particularly good about in school? Maybe the teacher would be willing to give a little extra attention.

Proving They're Okay: High Fives and Pats on the Back

As a primary intervention, these kids need to know they are okay. Remember, from a young age they have encountered and experienced some version of failure on a continual basis. Their core sense of self is defective. Down deep they truly believe something is terribly wrong. If this were not the case, why does everyone around them seem to get it, when they don't at all?

Recently, a sixteen-year-old spent much of the time sobbing while I reviewed his testing data. Surrounded by academic stars in a competitive suburban high school, he saw himself as stupid and disconnected from his peers. I reviewed his strengths to counterbalance his negative self-view. I pointed out the things he did well.

Our session was the first time anyone outside of his family had said anything like this to him. His sobs were sobs of relief from the weight of negative self-perceptions. A tremendous burden was being lifted from him. This understanding was only the beginning of his recognizing and then overcoming his sense of defectiveness.

Along with words given to children, we need to offer positive nonverbal signals and messages of encouragement. Don't underestimate the value of patting kids on the back and giving them high fives. This makes things fun for them and reinforces your connection. Without saying anything, you are saying, "You're doing great! Keep it up." It's amazing how motivating that can be.

This type of emotional encouragement is the only thing I know of in the academic arena that is keeping SDLs going. It is this thera-

peutic aspect of learning that motivates kids and keeps them connected. Without it, they are going to be irretrievably lost.

They have to know there are people beyond immediate family members who care uniquely about them. Key adults are needed who will take the time to connect with them on a regular basis, reinforcing the message that they are okay, something they have not felt for a long time.

Recently I observed a Little League coach pitching to a youngster who was clearly not a good hitter. The child must have missed sixty easy pitches in a row. Despite dreadfully hot weather, the coach persisted on patiently throwing ball after ball until the youngster got a hit. Afterward the coach made a point of walking over to the child. "Brandon, that was a great hit," he said. Punctuating success like this is essential for the SDL. They are so discouraged in general that anyone noticing their small successes is giving them enormous help in overcoming their negative perceptions.

The style of the encouraging coach is what the SDL needs to experience every day.

The Million Dollar Challenge:
Building a Deck or Reading a Book

In my work with SDLs, I try to counter their negative self-view by explaining they are not disabled and they are not damaged, something they deeply believe. I use the following story with teenagers almost verbatim:

"Imagine you're offered a million dollars to build a backyard deck. You're given basic diagrammatic directions, and all of the tools and materials. Do you think you could build the deck in a month?"

Typically the child says, "Absolutely. Yes — not a problem!" An easy million.

"Now I'll offer you the same million dollars to read a 500-page book and write a 15-page essay on the major aspects of the book. Again, I will give you a month to finish the project. Do you think you will get the million now?"

"No chance. It would be impossible."

"Now make me the same offer. I guarantee you by the end of the month the deck would be in shambles. I'd be very frustrated. The book would be finished, though, and the essay written."

"Now you tell me, which brain is better?"

I love this exercise because the kids get it. They comprehend that self-hating and berating are misguided. They're not defective, as they assumed. They simply don't function as well or as efficiently on certain tasks, such as reading and writing. For other tasks they function just fine, even better than others do.

It isn't as easy as it seems in this exercise, but the comparison of strengths and weaknesses helps put some things into perspective for the child. It helps them to see that they are not uniquely flawed. These kids have layers and layers of self-hatred, so one story won't fix all their problems. However, almost all SDLs that I tell this story to seem to feel better afterward.

School is an arena where many students formulate the idea that they are ineffective and dumb. School curriculum is heavily dominated by language processing, reading, and writing—one type of intelligence.

The predominant emphasis of language-processing skills through reading, writing, and spelling activities leads to erroneous assumptions (such as "I'm defective and dumb").

Structuring, Cuing, and Guiding

Shut-down learners need a lot of structuring, cuing, and guiding to help them manage in school. How does this work?

During testing, SDLs are asked to perform specific activities. Here's an example from the testing. On the cognitive test, the child is asked, "What should you do if you lose a toy belonging to one of your friends?"

A shut-down child answers, "Give it back to them."

"But you lost it," I reiterate.

The child again says, "Give it back to them."

With a little more cuing, such as asking for more information or clarification, she gets the idea and is able to articulate it: "Buy her a new one." Without the cuing, the answer would remain incomplete.

Here's another example. The same child is asked to name three different states of the U.S.

The child states, "New York City, Washington, Philadelphia, etc."

To cue the child I say, "Those are cities, I asked for states." Typically she then replies, "Oh, yeah, New York, Pennsylvania, New Jersey, etc."

Again, the cuing brings her out of her initial response. Without external structuring, the child would be unable to answer correctly on her own.

The same is true of SDLs' reading comprehension. If you listen to their answers to questions about what they have read, they are often vague and lacking adequate detail. There's a story on a test I give relating to gold miners and the method they used to pan for gold. For many children, this is the first time they've heard of gold miners, making the comprehension of the story difficult. When asked to explain the process of the miners, they often stare blankly, unable to recall the steps of the process. With some cuing or structuring, the answers often improve.

The SDL really cannot read extended text without adult interaction. Frequently, lost in a maze of words, they need cuing and anchoring to help them become oriented to what they are reading and the questions and demands placed on them.

STRUCTURING, CUING, GUIDING

- SDLs need help elaborating an answer or response to questions.
- If the child gives a vague response, guide the child with questions.

Structuring, cuing, and guiding help the SDL formulate more complete verbal answers.

The cuing provides a structure for their disorganized answers. It's like giving them a computer-based operating system.

Following Directions

Because SDLs often misunderstand questions and directions, it should never be assumed they understand what is expected of them. Teachers need to continually check in with them and get direct feedback about their understanding.

Checking is a major intervention with the SDL. For all of the reasons described earlier regarding their weak language systems, SDLs do not process information easily, especially spoken information. It should never be assumed such a child will follow spoken directions.

Physically going over to the child, talking with him, and making eye contact will help reduce frustration and anguish.

Sometimes teachers feel these accommodations and approaches are too difficult to carry out on top of the other demands placed upon them in the classroom. As stated earlier, there are many pressures put upon the teacher. Some of these interventions are easily done, though. It just takes the bell going off in the teacher's mind to remind him that the SDL will need a little cuing and orienting.

Most good teachers provide these accommodations naturally, but it helps to emphasize these points so that the teacher doesn't think the SDL child is simply being difficult or resistant. When the teacher understands an SDL's makeup better, her internal dialogue might go something like this: "Oh, yeah, Eric's a shut-down learner. He doesn't understand the directions. Let me go over to him after the class gets started. He will need my support to get him on board with the activity."

This thought process should occur every time a teacher interacts with a kid such as Eric. It's better to assume he doesn't understand the assignment or the activity. Again, the encouragement, the pat on the back, and cuing will bring him out of the shut-down mode.

Family Interventions

What do these children need from their family? They need the same thing they need in school. They need parents who understand them and do not get pulled into a battle of wills. The avoidance of angry interactions is a challenge for everyone. Most parents and children in these situations are engaged in tense, repetitive struggles. Changing these patterns can be extremely difficult.

> **HELPFUL TEACHER ACCOMMODATIONS**
> - Probably the most helpful accommodation is the friendly pat on the back with the statement, "How are you doing?"
> - Too often, SDLs sense intense disapproval from teachers. Going over to them and making sure the child is on board with you is enormously helpful. They won't come to you!

Many factors contribute to this difficulty. Much of the household tone is dependent upon how dejected and disconnected the child feels. If the child has given up, pervasive avoidance and shirking of day-to-day responsibilities will be the result. Household battles are inevitable; none however, improves the situation. SDL children have an incredibly difficult time functioning independently at home. They cannot complete assignments or household chores without excessive structured supervision.

The problem is that when parents give a considerable amount of supervision, the interaction frequently becomes a screaming match between parent and child. This volatile situation must be avoided at all costs to foster success for the SDL. Of course, yielding to the child's every whim can feed the child's self-centered perspective, adding to the sense of alienation and frustration in the household. So, what does work?

Communication Patterns in the Household

Parents need help learning how to communicate with their child. SDLs are very difficult to talk to about issues of concern. Negative and irritable patterns of communication play out in a habitual manner. Sometimes seeking the services of a therapist in your community who is well-versed in these issues will help you guide communication with

COMMUNICATING WITH CHILDREN

- Above all, try to take the tension out of the interaction.
- SDLs feel very badly about themselves, at their core.

Don't contribute to their sense of self-loathing.

your SDL child. The therapy should start with the realization that the child is not shut down purely because of motivational issues, rather, the child is shutting down for many good reasons. This realization takes the heat out of the communication cycle, and helps you start to see your child in a different light.

Parents are reminded about the deck-building exercise in the Million Dollar Challenge. Being aware of your child's strengths and weaknesses helps you understand that he is not shutting down in school purely because of emotional or motivational problems. The typical hypothesis put forth by the parent is "he can do it if he tries." This explanation puts the blame on the child's motivation. But the child is unmotivated not purely because of lack of effort. This understanding is crucial for parents.

Parents tend to adopt punishing postures with children who don't appear to be motivated. This approach is a mistake, leading to greater degrees of anger and increased shutting down. Parents must be taught to understand the interactions taking place.

I am not suggesting that limits be removed altogether, but it is the tone of punishment that needs to be addressed. Punishment has the effect of choking the child even more than he feels from his day-to-day school interactions. The child places blame squarely on the parents to deflect any sense of personal responsibility. He typically adopts a blaming posture rather than looking at his own behavior.

Parents who believe they have absolutely no control over their difficult child may feel a sense of momentary victory after punishing him. This feeling is almost always short-lived, as the child rarely assumes greater degrees of responsibility as a result of the punishment. The desired end point, that the child will become self-directing, is almost never achieved this way. Parents rely on punishment because it is their last attempt to grasp control.

Another typical problem is the finger-pointing that takes place in the household between parents. As a result of ongoing years of frustration and difficulty, parents are frequently polarized in their relationship. Marital communication is challenging enough without the variable of an extremely difficult shut-down child. In the dance between the parents and the shut-down child, usually one parent feels he has the right approach and if the other parent would only listen and do it his way, all problems would be solved.

Typically the stricter parent believes his way will lead to the solution of the child's problems. This parent accuses the other parent of feeding into the child's demands rather than helping. As there may be a grain of truth in this, the softer (more indulgent) parent usually reacts by countering the stricter parent's punishing style. The

accommodating parent sees the stricter parent as too harsh, irritable, and reactive and attempts to buffer the child from the stricter
parent.

When listening to these interactions, which often escalate into
battles, I can see that each parent brings a certain amount of truth
to the table. If the stricter parent lightens up, the child will typically
feel relief. If the more indulgent parent tightens the reins, the child
will feel he has to be held accountable.

It is incredibly difficult for parents to find this middle-ground
approach because of all the fighting and finger-pointing. The harsh-
er parent feels disgusted and enraged, while the supposedly indulgent parent feels alienated and isolated. Marital problems many
times deepen as the communication becomes increasingly frayed
and tense.

INEFFECTIVE PUNISHMENTS

Punishments are generally ineffective. Ones to avoid in particular are:

- Long harangues
- Idle threats
- Excessive use of timeouts

Punishments will aim their anger toward you rather than make the child feel badly about what he's done.

Blaming between the parents leads to a sense of depletion that can't be ignored. It is my observation that the mother within a two-parent family is the one who typically feels most depleted by the child's stance in the household. Mothers come into my office feeling wrung out and worn down. Because the child has been unresponsive to various attempts at bringing about changes, the mother feels like a failure. The anger, often rage, between the parents compounds the SDL's sense of alienation. The chaotic anger weakens the family system. The child does not see anyone in control at the top.

In effect, the captain has stepped down from managing the ship, and no one is in charge. For the SDL, this is perilous. These children already lack an adequate steering mechanism, so a captainless ship will cause them to flounder even more.

In one case I encountered a mother depleted and exhausted by her attempts to get the youngster to act more responsibly. It was a daily struggle to get him out of bed. His motivation was extremely low, and the mother's experience was one of rejection. She felt she had failed her child and her family. To help her child, the mother needed to regain her sense of herself and her family. A parent's loss of confidence and alienation is common in these situations.

This loss of parental energy is the exact opposite of what the SDL needs, because they are already operating on low energy. As I have suggested, it is in the relationship with key adults, parents, and teachers where these youngsters can feel and experience something qualitatively different. If this positive relationship does not happen, their low energy and sense of dejection compound the problem. They sink further into a morass of lower levels of responsibility. They retreat to computers and video games because they are in their medium of comfort. These activities do not involve facing real demands and responsibilities.

Help for the Fathers

Often it's the fathers who become enraged at the SDL and the dynamic between the mother and the SDL. They accuse the mother of indulging the child. The fathers sometimes give up at this juncture. They retreat into a sport or hobby such as golf, fishing, or the Internet. They feel they tried and are washing their hands of the situation. The child feels rejected from the father as a result. Blowups are frequently the only form of interaction taking place between the father, or the stricter parent, and child.

This pattern of father-child relating needs a change. Finding a common ground is helpful. SDLs like the outdoors and many other hands-on activities, so engaging them in an activity they like and sharing it with them helps relieve the tension.

A very angry shut-down teenager came into my office. The father and teenager were clashing over almost everything. After one session, the father was encouraged to perceive the child differently and to look for common ground. Viewing the child in a different light was not easy to do, because they remained polarized in their

positions. The son saw the father as a punitive tyrant. The father saw the child as completely out of control and impossible to manage. Both enjoyed a common hobby of motorcycles and building engines. Over the weekend they were given an assignment to not talk about school at all or any other household responsibility. They were to simply share an activity they enjoyed together. The child and father decided to rebuild the son's motorcycle engine.

A week later the mother sent in a letter saying her son's disposition had changed dramatically. He was a much more pleasant individual around the house and more responsive to the parents' requests.

While this relationship cannot change permanently from one weekend's interaction, it was the start of changing the way the family dealt with each other. Frozen patterns of communication were changed by finding common ground.

It is important to emphasize that stubbornness and irritability are typically a part of the SDL package. The frustration and failure

---

FATHERS, DON'T RETREAT!

Fathers are very important in countering the negative emotions of the SDL.

- Find shared interests and hobbies with the child.
- Don't talk about school while engaged in the activity.
- Watch that you don't become confrontational.
- Help lighten things up.

---

experienced are not isolated to school but carry over into the household. As interactions and relations become strained, the children become more oppositional and defiant.

These problems are compounded if there are other children in the family who might or might not have the characteristic qualities of the SDL. I work with many families in which one child of three, for example, is the high-spatial child who detests school, surrounded by siblings who are succeeding.

This family dynamic further intensifies the child's rage and feeling of failure and low self-esteem. The other children find school gratifying and receive more positive interactions from parents and teachers. Invariably comparisons occur, even though parents may bend over backward to not make such immediate comparisons. These comparisons result in the child's sense that she is unloved. Normal sibling tensions become magnified and intensified.

It behooves parents in such a situation to spend time understanding the nature of this child and finding ways of having her experience success and a sense of well-being.

I worked with a family and encouraged the dad to take the child on a solo camping trip. While some may object that the other children would feel angry about this special treatment, the net effect was a lessening of tensions all around. The other children were relieved

and happy to have the more challenging youngster out of the house for a period of time, while the difficult SDL and his father had a great experience together.

Type I Reading Remediation

The interventions and suggestions in this section and the next focus on the academic functioning of the SDL.

There are five major components to the reading process. These are:

- Phonemic awareness
- Decoding
- Reading fluency
- Vocabulary
- Comprehension

Children who struggle with the first three elements are what I call Type I readers. By far, these children have the most common learning problems found in school. Their fundamental problem is difficulty efficiently decoding printed words. In other words, their phonics skills are weak.

The remediations that help overcome these weaknesses are the multisensory methods mentioned earlier, known as the Orton-Gillingham approaches (www.ortonacademy.org, www.wilsonlanguage.com). These approaches are high structured, sequential, and multisensory, engaging the senses simultaneously. There are a number of them on the market.

MULTISENSORY METHODS
(ORTON-GILLINGHAM APPROACHES)

The multisensory methods share a number of characteristics. They tend to be:

- More hands-on, actively engaging the child's various senses of visual, auditory, tactile simultaneously
- Sequential, with one skill leading to the next
- Arranged in a highly controlled sequence

Multisensory methods are the most effective for anyone struggling with decoding (phonics).

Developing Reading Fluency

Type I readers also need help with the development of reading fluency as an important part of their remediation. Remember, these children tend to read in a slow, labored, word-by-word manner. They lack a basic understanding of how reading sounds because of their characteristic style of reading, which is very laborious, slow, and choppy.

Reading fluency training is like practicing a piece of music. You may know the chords, but you don't play them very smoothly. The

> **FLUENCY**
>
> Reading fluency problems are at the core of many SDLs' avoidance and dislike of reading. To improve reading fluency:
>
> - Engage children with repeated reading activities, where they practice a selection out loud for a minute or two until they are almost 100 percent fluent.
> - Help kids understand that reading is like a sports skill. They must practice it enough over time for it to get better.
>
> Keep practice sessions short (5-10 minutes).

only answer is to play the chords over and over until they become automatically and fully internalized.

The same is true for reading fluency. With repeated reading practice under controlled conditions, children internalize the rhythm of the language and the flow of a reading passage.

At the Cooper Learning Center, one of the nicer aspects of the fluency program using Great Leaps (www.greatleaps.com) is the bonding that takes place between parent and child. Even the older kids in high school who are being trained in reading fluency seem to really enjoy the parental attention that results from this reward-based program.

Type II Reading Remediation

Type II readers do not have difficulty with phonics or reading fluency, but they have trouble understanding text.

Type II readers need direct training in comprehension. Lindamood Bell Learning Processes' called "Visualizing & Verbalizing for Language Comprehension and Thinking" (www.lindamood-bell.com) is a perfect match for these youngsters. In this method, children are taught to actively visualize what they are reading from the word to the sentence and paragraph level. This skill is directly taught in a multisensory fashion.

In Visualizing and Verbalizing, the child is trained to actively visualize what he is reading about by forming pictures in his mind. Specific questions about the text guide the reader to formulate pictures. Over time, the child does this more automatically on his own.

Too often, comprehension is taught by having kids answer worksheet questions. Worksheets do not teach reading comprehension, and they have little value in remediation. They do not directly teach a skill. Children are being worksheeted to death. Worksheets are particularly loathsome to shut-down learners, who find them an endless bore. Overemphasis on worksheets without multisensory engagement of the child leads to the disconnection and shut-down posture of these youngsters. Unfortunately, the kids come to my center showing all of the worksheets they had to complete in a week. They're drowning in a sea of premade busy work having nothing to do with their needs or learning style.

IS YOUR CHILD A DISCONNECTED READER?

Reading is a difficult process for many children. Listen to your child reading. Watch for these signs to see if your child is a disconnected reader:

- Out-loud reading is done in a halting, laborious tone.
- The reading is very word by word.
- There is little flow.
- There are many pauses and hesitancies.
- The child sounds like she does not understand.
- If the answer is yes to these questions, fluency training would probably be very helpful.

In a method such as Visualizing and Verbalizing, kids are trained to think in a different way by simultaneously stimulating different senses. This gets the disconnected child more actively involved. It's a better fit for their learning style.

Good, flexible comprehension skills typically do not come naturally to the SDL. Comprehension skills need to be developed individually and in very small groups for these children. Small groups allow for strong emotional encouragement from teachers, which is imperative. Similar approaches should be taken to develop writing and study skills. Skills need to be taught in a multisensory fashion so the child is more engaged in the learning process.

One of the best books I have encountered to help parents understand the importance of reading comprehension and how to develop it in children who are struggling is *7 Keys to Comprehension: How to Help Your Kids Read It and Get It!*, by Susan Zimmermann and Chryse Hutchins. This book emphasizes the need to:

- *Create mental images:* Good readers create a wide range of visual, auditory, and other sensory images as they read, and they become emotionally involved with what they read.

- *Use background knowledge:* Good readers use their relevant prior knowledge before, during, and after reading to enhance their understanding of what they're reading.
- *Ask questions:* Good readers generate questions before, during, and after reading to clarify meaning, make predictions, and focus their attention on what's important.
- *Make inferences:* Good readers use their prior knowledge and information from what they read to make predictions, seek answers to questions, draw conclusions, and create interpretations that deepen their understanding of the text.
- *Determine the most important ideas or themes:* Good readers identify key ideas or themes as they read, and they can distinguish between important and unimportant information.
- *Synthesize information:* Good readers track their thinking as it evolves during reading, to get the overall meaning.
- *Use fix-up strategies:* Good readers are aware of when they understand and when they don't. If they have trouble understanding specific words, phrases, or longer passages, they use a wide range of problem-solving strategies, including skipping ahead, rereading, asking questions, using a dictionary, and reading the passage aloud.

Vocabulary Development

As stated earlier, this is a typically weak skill for SDLs. Their word understanding and usage are limited. A lack of vocabulary seriously impacts one's ability to understand material that is encountered. Michael Graves, a researcher in the field of reading, talks about the concept of word consciousness. Word consciousness refers to awareness of and interest in words and their meaning. SDLs have "tin ears" for language, as you will recall from the earlier discussion.

DEVELOPING VOCABULARY AT HOME

Vocabulary development is crucial to many aspects of reading and writing. SDLs do not have well-developed word awareness or word consciousness. To develop this, do the following:

- Consult one of the essential vocabulary books on the market (see appendix).
- Each week add about ten new words.
- Put each word on an index card.
- Have the child draw a picture illustrating the word on the front of the card. For example, for the word impede, the child could draw a stick figure of a person trying to get by an obstacle of some kind.
- Have the child color the picture with markers.
- On the back side, have the child write the definition of the word in her own language.
- Place the cards in a box or on a ring.
- Review the words frequently with the child.

This is not a juvenile or childish method. When my daughter was a junior and senior in high school, she used this approach, and it greatly helped her to internalize very difficult and challenging SAT words.

Word consciousness does not come easily to them. Graves has developed a four-part program for fostering vocabulary development. This program emphasizes wide reading, teaching individual words, teaching word-learning strategies, and fostering word consciousness. (See Graves, M.F. & Watts-Taffe, S.M. (2002). The Place of word consciousness in a research-based vocabulary program. In Farstrup, A.E. & Samuels, S.J. (Eds), *What Research Has To Say About Reading Instruction* (3rd ed), Newark, DE, International Reading Association.)

The Cooper Learning Center also has piloted a home-based vocabulary program. The boxed text on this page illustrates how to develop and practice the words.

Reducing the Mountain

While emphasizing that homework can be very troublesome, the parent needs to break down the material so it is more manageable for the youngster. To SDL children, normal amounts of homework and reading assignments look like a mountain, and they are at the foot of this mountain craning their necks to look up to the top. They usually cannot see the top of the mountain, because it's so high and surrounded by a bank of clouds. However, the parent can help them climb it by breaking down the work and assignments and setting up a reasonable structure with smaller goals. This reduction makes the material more digestible and increases the likelihood that the child will have a degree of success.

REDUCING THE MOUNTAIN

Kids look at their assignments as insurmountable mountains.

- Find ways to break the assignment into small digestible parts.
- Work out a timetable to complete the smaller parts.
- Over time, the child will do this more on his own.

Take any reading or assignment that your child must complete. Divide it into portions and set up a reasonable timeline for the child to follow. The mountain won't be so impossible to scale.

Outside Tutoring

SDL children also tend to benefit from outside tutorial support. Good tutoring is like receiving learning therapy. Many SDLs' self-esteem improves dramatically when they receive the right kind of attention from such a tutor, who functions much like the coach described earlier.

Such tutors (or learning therapists) focus on specific skill areas and accomplish different goals. Again, training the children with multisensory methodologies and actively engaging the youngster are the remedial vehicles to break the cycle of negativity and pervasive discouragement. Utilizing the Orton-Gillingham methods for kids with decoding problems or the approaches mentioned earlier for reading comprehension is often the best way to address each component of the reading process.

Tutoring or learning therapy also allows for a great deal of emotional support and a considerable amount of pats on the back. It's crucial for these children to hear sincere encouragement on a regular basis. These children are starved for this type of attention. Like plants that have received no water or sunlight, they are withering. When remediation and coaching work, these once-wilted plants stand tall and flourish. They exude confidence and energy.

Assistive Technology

When I discuss different ways to help their SDL child, I highlight two major directions for parents to consider. The first centers on direct interventions (tutoring, therapy) and the second discusses ways to get around the problem (accommodations and use of assistive technology). Because of assistive technology, there has never been a better time to have a learning problem.

The most important aspect of assistive technology is that the child needs training on how to use the software. It should not be assumed that because the child is of the modern generation, he will naturally gravitate to it. The child needs to understand how the software can really help him so he sees the benefit and uses it regularly (and not because he is being nagged by his parents). Once the

---

**HOW TO FIND GOOD TUTORS AND
KNOW THEIR METHODS ARE SUPPORTED**

The first step is to know what you are trying to remediate. For example, is the child primarily a Type I (phonics/decoding/reading fluency issues) or Type II (reading comprehension/vocabulary development) child?

- Once you've determined what your child's needs are, start with word of mouth in your area.
- Ask the tutor if she knows specialized approaches for treating the specific problem areas.

Write down the method. Check with respected professionals in the community who deal with these problems to find out more about the suggested method. Is the method supported by research?

---

child is using the technology, he is in a position to take greater responsibility for his learning.

This concept of taking responsibility for one's learning is a major step for SDLs and not one that is easy to accomplish. Assistive technology can make a big difference in becoming an independent, self-regulating student.

There are many different software programs on the market. Because these are changing rapidly, I will not mention any specifically. For helpful information on assistive technology, go to www.ldonline.org. When on this site, go to the "In Depth" section to access descriptions of the various software programs available.

Medication

Parents come to my office ambivalent and unsure about treating their child with medication. They will typically have gone on the Internet to read about many medication issues, which can add to their confusion.

There is a tendency on the part of professionals and parents to seek quick fixes. Certainly if medication provides benefits and immediate relief, there is a sense that it is the answer.

As the children get older, treating them with medication seems to become increasingly more difficult. When children who are struggling in school arrive in my office, which is typically by the time they are in the middle school grades, medication has been tried to some degree, with varying levels of success. When they reach high school, many children increasingly resist the notion of taking medication, even if there are perceived benefits. It is their sense that the medication is another attempt at controlling them, which leads to greater resistance to taking it and going along with the doctor's recommendations.

Assuming that we are talking about stimulant medication, which is commonly used to treat ADHD, if the medication does work, its primary purpose is to help the child focus and pay attention more consistently. This approach can provide some relief and might help the SDL be attentive and more available in the classroom. However, the child may be focusing better while maintaining all other skill area weaknesses described earlier, so the medication will not take care of these deficiencies. I tell parents it's like a person who has a flawed golf swing taking medication. They may be paying attention better, but there are stills flaws in their swing.

SDLs are certainly not operating on all cylinders in school. I explain to parents that if a youngster is to function successfully, he typically needs six out of eight cylinders in school. The SDL is operating with two cylinders, at best, in a school setting. If medication has the effect of adding a cylinder or two, this can be very positive for the child. However, all of the issues described earlier still need to be addressed.

Communication, understanding, and providing the right skills remain essential to the SDL. These variables must be addressed.

Jack: A Classic Shut-Down Learner

The following is a summary of an evaluation that I conducted with Jack and his parents, Susan and Stuart.

Introduction

Jack is a thirteen-year-old child who had just completed the sixth grade at the time he came in to my office. The parents provided a history that was similar to so many of the SDL children I have seen over the years.

For the first four grades, no one identified that Jack had any type of reading disability. As Jack's parents noted, "The school said he was fine. It was all his attitude."

By fourth grade, Jack's behavior started to decline. The school finally tested him and found that he was functioning on a mid-first-grade level for reading, spelling, and writing. His parents started Jack on outside tutoring, with someone who was familiar with multisensory structured language methods. This started to help, but the school curriculum was going too fast for Jack, and his functioning in school rapidly declined. Jack's sixth-grade year was very difficult and his parents lost patience. They brought him in for an assessment because they wanted to know whether his learning problems were related to his behavior and attitudinal problems. They consulted with their pediatrician, who advised them to have this assessment to help determine some sort of direction for him.

To give you a flavor of Jack, I will offer the parents' responses to many of the questions they completed in questionnaires.

QUESTION: What is the reason for this referral for an assessment?

PARENT RESPONSE: He's always angry and he has behavior problems in school.

QUESTION: What concerns you most about your child?

PARENT RESPONSE: Anger. Always needs to be in charge.

QUESTION: Describe the best things about your child.

PARENT RESPONSE: Sensitive, loving, and tries to do well. He will help out when needed. He is very honest.

QUESTION: Identify and describe any specific academic strengths.

PARENT RESPONSE: Math and anything hands-on.

QUESTION: Indicate the child's special talents, interests, or athletic activities.

PARENT RESPONSE: Building things, cooking, wrestling, and hockey.

Characteristics Described on a Checklist by Parents

The following are the concerning characteristics identified by his parents to describe Jack:

- Poor schoolwork
- Self-conscious and easily embarrassed
- Showing off or clowning

- Stubborn, sullen, and/or irritable
- Unhappy, sad, or depressed
- Argues a lot
- Actively defies or refuses to comply with adult requests
- Bragging, boasting
- Touchy/easily annoyed by others
- Blames others for his mistakes or misbehaviors
- Feels inferior to others
- Easily frustrated in efforts
- Unaware of errors in his performance
- Fails to give close attention to details and/or makes careless mistakes in schoolwork or other activities
- Difficulty engaging in tasks that require sustained mental effort
- Cries easily
- Frequent physical complaints

Assessment of Jack

The assessment process began in the waiting room with the first handshake. This is where I got my first glimpse of what the child was like and how he was going to respond, at least initially, to the notion of an assessment. I met Jack in the summer, so already the deck was stacked against his being willing to come in for this evaluation. Kids are happier when they are going to miss school for the testing.

As I anticipated, Jack showed very little emotion when I went to greet him. I made a joke about his looking miserable, and this interaction seemed to lighten him up slightly.

Back in my office, Jack and I started conversing. He told me that he was into wrestling and that this takes up a great deal of his time. He also informed me that he and a friend were building a tree house in the woods near their house. I asked Jack how he knew how to do build the tree house. Jack stated, "We had a deck built in our backyard and I just watched. This gave me a lot of ideas about how to do it."

When I asked Jack about school, he told me "it stinks." It was Jack's perception that his teacher was always on his case and that he was not given any real support, "even though I had an IEP [Individualized Education Plan]." Jack appeared to be very aware of accommodations that he was supposedly going to be given in the classroom because of his IEP, and it was his perception that he received very little support.

The data that I derived showed Jack to be very true to form in terms of the classic SDL characteristics. He was exceptional when putting blocks together to match different spatial patterns, scoring in the 98th percentile. In fact, he was able to complete every item successfully on this measure, which goes up to nearly seventeen years of age. Further, Jack was able to analyze a series of different matrix patterns and designs, showing very clear visual analytic skills.

At some point in the middle of the assessment, I turned to Jack and said, "I know what you're about. You're a Lego kid."

Jack smiled and seemed to understand right away. I explained to Jack that many of the kids who do well with these tasks typically do not like to read, spell, or write. Jack nodded enthusiastically in agreement.

Jack's reading was classic of the Type I variety that I described earlier. Jack was asked by me to read words aloud from a list to assess his decoding skills. Some of the words with which he struggled included:

- evening
- passage

- receive
- gasoline
- calendar
- human
- important
- institute

These words were either totally misread ("rekive" for receive) or guessed at with a close substitute ("everything" for evening). Jack started having significant difficulty with words within a fourth-grade range.

Jack also struggled greatly with different nonsense words (fup, loonip, ligh) and he was extremely inefficient with the names that were presented. Jack could read some of the names on the list, but these were the most basic names and he read them extremely slowly and inefficiently.

I then asked Jack to read in context from different passages. This oral reading provides a real window into the process of reading and how the child conducts himself while reading. Jack's reading of selections within the fourth- and fifth-grade levels was quite choppy, inefficient, and laborious. His reading was not smooth at all, like driving down a dirt road with many potholes. Clearly, reading was an overwhelmingly tedious act for him. Substitution errors in the text interfered with Jack's capacity to process and understand the material. For example, Jack substituted the word "forest" for farthest, "desert" for deserted and "unrooted" for uprooted. Obviously, such substitutions altered the meaning of the text a great deal. Within the fifth-grade level I noted that Jack was showing "extreme insecurity, hacking through the passage." It was very clear why Jack detested reading.

As is true with almost all SDLs, their spelling and writing skills are quite revealing. The following are the errors that Jack made with his spelling:

- light/lite
- circle/circul
- correct/cerect
- minute/minet
- ruin/rouwen
- believe/beleav
- train/trane
- watch/wach
- result/resolt
- educate/egcate

Jack was also asked to write a story about a picture that is part of a psychological test known as the Thematic Apperception Test. In the picture (briefly mentioned earlier with Matthew), a boy is looking at a violin, and he doesn't seem particularly happy. It is very interesting to see how the child creates a story about the boy and the violin. Will the boy practice and learn to become a world-class violinist? Will he break the violin in frustration and avoid learning to play the instrument at all? Are his parents seen as supportive or do they conflict with him? The possibilities and outcomes are endless.

Besides giving us an example of the child's writing abilities, the story tends to pull forth emotional content about the child's self-concept and his willingness to work through frustration to reach a goal. When I read one of these stories to a child's parents, they are often amazed by how the story reveals their child's issues.

Jack's story is transcribed exactly as it was written, leaving his spelling and sentence structure problems in place. I have added Jack's intended word in brackets wherever it's particularly unclear.

Jack's Violin Story

One day a little boy about 10 years old fond [found] a big chonck of wood. This boy loved to lisen to music and always wanted to play an instermint but what he emiiered [admired] was the vialen. So this boy thote it would be a good idea if he made one with that blok of wood. So he needed tools but he had no money. So he went out and collected cans and some more cans and when he got enof cans he went and traded them in for money so he went and boat [bought] a chisel and harmer [hammer] some violen strings and some nails. So this boy went to work he worked night and day to make it and when he finished he was so happy but then when he went to play it he did not no [know] how so he sat down and thote [thought] of an idea. The End

The story is very interesting on many levels. Certainly on the mechanical/spelling level, the errors reveal the level of disability that Jack faces and the degree of frustration, considering that he is a seventh grader of above-average intelligence. Further, Jack's understanding of sentence structure clearly was quite limited.

On the psychological level, the story also is interesting in that the main character uses some of the best traits of the SDL. He finds creative solutions, going as far as to build a violin out of a block of wood. As I got to know Jack, I saw that this would not be a preposterous notion, and it was one that he probably would see as possible, given his abilities with building. The boy's inability to play the instrument at the end is symbolic of Jack's ongoing difficulty with academics and not being able to "play the music" in school. Jack's story ends somewhat abruptly, without a solution as to how he will overcome this inability. In all likelihood, this is how he feels about his ongoing difficulty with reading, spelling, and writing. Jack has had tutors, yet he continues to struggle greatly and is on the verge of giving up and shutting down in school.

The Feedback Conference

Following the evaluation, I met with Jack's parents to review my findings and impressions. During the testing, I had shared a rough draft of the manuscript of this book to get their impressions and to give them an idea as to how I was conceptualizing Jack. When I came into the office where they were looking at the manuscript, they excitedly exclaimed that I had nailed Jack exactly in my description of the shut-down learner. The following is a transcription of the session that we had after the testing.

RICHARD SELZNICK: What's your reaction to what you read in the book? Does it seem to fit him?

SUSAN: It fits him very well. He certainly was a Lego kid.

RS: I saw it in the testing data. He's so much better nonverbally. He scored almost off the charts on the task called Block Design. This is one of the best measures of nonverbal intelligence that we have. His job was to put together blocks to match different patterns. The designs get really difficult and increase in significant complexity. These tests are designed for kids in the range of six to seventeen years old. Jack was able to get a perfect performance. That's in the 98th percentile compared to other kids his age. His performance completely reinforced the notion that Jack is a very spatial and visually based kid.

Then he did a task called Matrix Reasoning in which he had to analyze different visual patterns that, again, increase in complexity. He scored nicely on this task as well.

When you put both of these tasks together it suggests that Jack's nonverbal ability would be very high, basically in the superior range.

His verbal abilities were okay — they certainly weren't efficient, but they were much closer to average and a bit below average. You see a real discrepancy between his nonverbal, or spatial, intelligence in comparison to his verbal abilities.

He also did very nicely on another nonverbal task that I gave him in which he had to copy a number of different shapes and designs and organize them on the page. His designs were accurately copied and they were well-spaced, reinforcing my assessment of his nonverbal ability. He was also able to recall eight of the designs from memory, which is considered very good. He has a good visual awareness and visual memory.

SUSAN: Yes, we see this with him all the time. Did he tell you that he is building a tree house in the woods with his friends? He's doing a very nice job. It's very impressive. Also, he's doing it all on his own.

What were some of the weaknesses that you found in the assessment?

RS: The flip side of the coin is his reading disability, or dyslexia, and it is puzzling that anyone is even questioning whether this exists at all. To me it's a slam dunk that he is dyslexic. He is really hurting in reading, spelling, and writing. This is affecting his self-esteem, his sense of self-concept, really everything.

STU: I thought dyslexia was when you see things upside down and backward. Does he do that?

RS: That notion of seeing backward is one of the great misunderstandings about dyslexia. Jack doesn't see upside down or backward, but he translates the print on the page incredibly inefficiently. He substitutes words that don't belong and it greatly alters the meaning. When he reads it's like he's listening to a radio with a good deal of static. It would be very hard to get the information that way. Essentially, that is what dyslexia is and it affects everything that he does. Needless to say it also affects his writing and spelling. Further, his whole sense of self-esteem and security are greatly affected.

STU: Yes, I believe that much of the behavior that we see is a direct result of all of this that you're talking about.

RS: The kid is a sensitive enough kid and I can tell that if someone related to him in a certain way and didn't get down on him, that he would probably respond pretty well. He is clearly going to take a certain kind of handling given all the different variables. The problem is he is so down on himself because of his issues with reading and writing. He is becoming exactly what I describe in the book — he's shutting down. He's a classic shut-down learner. As I indicated, these problems become most pronounced in upper elementary school into middle school and that is what is happening with Jack. I'm sure he's not giving teacher-pleasing behaviors (mother nods in agreement) and he's probably looking quite bored and disconnected in class.

STU: Right. You'd probably see him talking back and looking disrespectful and not into it at all.

RS: It's a vicious cycle. I saw it in the waiting room when I went out to introduce myself to him. He certainly would not have been described as pleasant when I met him. His demeanor did not convey that he wanted to be here even a little bit. I joked with him some in the session and complimented him, and he seemed to respond somewhat better. I also tried to show him that he is a visually and spatially oriented kid, and this idea was something that he related to right away. With these kids the formula is really to show them an understanding of their issues, and that's hard.

SUSAN: Right. He puts up such a front, and he can be so difficult that it makes people not take the time to understand him.

RS: Correct. He is a spatial and visual learner, and he is disabled in core areas of reading, spelling, and writing. So anytime he is going to be asked to do those tasks in school, it's going to be a huge, huge burden for him. You know, I asked him whether he was getting help in school and he answered, "No, not really." He was pretty honest. He said, "I have an IEP. They're supposed to read things to me and give me extra time, but they usually don't do that for me."

STU: We had a problem this year. He was supposed to be getting in-class support because they feel he doesn't need more direct remediation. He was supposed to be getting a lot of accommodations, and from our point of view he wasn't getting them. We kept going to them, and it was getting very frustrating. When we had to sign the new IEP, we had them spell everything out to make sure that he would get what he needs next year.

SUE: The problem is that they perceive him to be very intelligent so they think he doesn't need support. As you can see from your own assessment, this is not true at all. We know that he's intelligent — that's not the issue. He falls behind very quickly and can't keep up with the work that they give him. You should see him try to manage the assignments. It's impossible. He can't complete the work. It's not only a function of time. Much of it is due to the fact that he can't process the information or translate the larger words in the text.

STU: He shuts down just like you said. As soon as he can't handle a problem, "Boom, I'm out of here." He's done. That's it.

SUSAN: A lot of the time he's compensating, even when he can't do it. This wears him down though. They really haven't addressed his disability — everything is compensation.

I tried to explain to his teachers how Jack is, but they see me as a mother who is simply taking up for her child and is not really looking at the truth.

STU: I don't think that people understand him in the way that you're suggesting he needs to be understood. That's a major problem. People don't know how to handle him. They don't guess that when you ask him to spell a word or to read in front of the class, that he can't do it and that he's going to be embarrassed by this, which will then lead to the misbehaving. You know, you get the snickers from the other kids, and that makes him want to crawl under a rock. He'll do anything to not be called upon in class.

SUSAN: Then he would get so embarrassed in one class that this would affect him in the other class. This happens quite a bit. He would be disruptive and then take it to the next class. You know he can be really nice, and he always wants to help people.

RS: That describes this kind of kid too, you know. They love to help out. Give him tasks and jobs and things that he can get done and he'd be great. That is one of the most important things you can do for him. Letting him do those kinds of things gives him tremendous reinforcement and self-esteem in ways that he is not getting in other places.

SUSAN: He also loves to cook and he's very good at it.

STU: There's so much that he likes to do, but put a book in front of him, forget about it.

RS: It's good that he's getting tutored and that they're using the multisensory Orton methods with him. The focus needs to be on developing his reading fluency and improving his decoding skills. His understanding of the text was pretty good when the material was read to him. He doesn't seem to have much of a comprehension problem. This is classic with dyslexia. I think that if he came in for reading fluency and continued with his tutoring, that this would make an impact on him. It's not easy or quick work, though. The

Orton-Gillingham programs tend to be effective, but they do take a long time.

SUSAN: The tutor has done a very nice job with him. She brought him from the first-grade level to where he is now. He still has a long way to go, but I think she's doing the right thing. She's also very encouraging and supportive of him.

RS: Along with the tutoring, we will get him started on a home-based program that will specifically target his reading fluency. This will involve his doing five-minute exercises at home each night over the course of a year. We've tracked many kids in this kind of program and those who have stayed with it have done very nicely. The fluency program will work well with the tutoring, as both will really be targeting the areas of need. They should give him much greater confidence in school. The fluency work should go hand in hand with the multisensory work that he is receiving from his tutor.

SUSAN: Do you think the gap will ever close with him?

RS: Look, being totally blunt and honest, even with good support and remediation, reading will probably always be a struggle for him. It's going to be a hard road for him. When you're hardwired this way, as he seems to be, reading, spelling, and writing will be a great struggle. It's probably inherited, just like the good traits and abilities that he has. The ultimate ticket is to build on the strengths that he has. I know that he can become depressed about his weaknesses and school can grind him down, but if you continue to focus on what he does well, this should help pull him through. We have to keep him from getting too down on himself so that he doesn't become completely shut down. He needs to hear messages of competence and that he is capable, over and over again, in spite of the difficulties. Then you have to steer him a certain way, to a certain type of job or profession that would be good for him, perhaps culinary school or some other area that he's attracted to exploring.

SUSAN: Do you think that he needs anger management?

RS: I think that if he feels understood and thinks that people are behind him, that should relieve him of much of his anger.

STU: I do too. I believe that almost all of his anger is related to the disability you talked about today.

RS: You do a little bit of the fluency training, you continue with tutoring, and have him come in and talk about what's going on in school. This combination should provide him with a fair amount of relief and support. I'd also like to see how he would do with certain assistive technology. There are great programs on the market that will make the reading process available to him on computer. Remember books on tape? Now it's books on computer. The computer will read the story to him as he follows along.

You also have to stay in close contact with the tutor. If I were you, I would email her on a regular basis to find out how he's doing and get feedback from her. This also gives you an opportunity to offer the tutor ideas and understanding from your perspective. You want to know how he's managing his emotions and dealing with his frustration, but the tutor also needs to be sensitive about not overly frustrating him and understanding when he is in over his head. It's going to be a long road under the best of circumstances.

SUSAN: What about medication? Do you think we should consider it?

RS: You know, it may help him to some extent. He certainly rates very high on difficulty with paying attention and being distractible. Hopefully, you see that his poor focusing is related to all of the skill issues that we discussed. I think that medication may provide him with some sense of relief, although you have to understand that most kids his age are pretty uncomfortable with the idea of it. They think that the medication will change their personality or control them.

*(At this point, Jack came into this session and
I started talking to him about the results.)*

RS: I talked to your parents about some of the things that I told you before. You're a smart kid. I think, though, that your experience in school makes you feel like you're not smart, because of the reading and spelling problems that you have to deal with every day. (Jack nods in agreement.)

I know you're a smart kid because you had a perfect performance with those blocks and you were great with a lot of those different visual patterns that I showed you. That is not something that I would take lightly. Those were tough tests. You got a perfect performance! This test goes up to seventeen years old!

You know, you're building a tree house and you do a lot of things really well. You have great visual awareness like we discussed before. You understood when I talked to you about being a Lego kid. Now, on the other side, your reading brain doesn't work nearly as well, so we're going to try to help you with that.

I know you have a good tutor and that's great. You have to stay with that. Getting better with reading is just like a sports skill. If you want to become a better wrestler, what do you have to do?

JACK: Practice.

RS: Exactly. You know if you want to beat that kid you told me about you have to work at it, right? (Jack laughs.) Reading is a skill, just like wrestling. You have to work at it, even though it's going to be something that you probably are going to hate. So we're going to get you working on exercises at home that you can do a few nights a week. We're also going to check in with your tutor to see how you're doing and then you and your parents will come in once in a while and we can talk about it and maybe help you to cope with the situation better.

SUSAN: Can you bring up the idea of the medication?

RS: We probably will have you talk with your physician about trying medication. This may help you focus a little better. You really are up against a lot given all of the things that we talked about and medication may give you a certain percentage of improvement. My concern would be that you may think that doing that will take care of everything. It just doesn't work that way.

(At this point, I always ask the kids if they have any questions.
True to form with every kid I've ever worked with, Jack had none.)

The Shut-Down
Learner's Perspective

Over the years, I have met many shut-down learners. Their stories are always compelling. The three interviews that follow were conducted after most of this book was written. The interviewees were asked to read a draft of the book and to offer comments from their perspectives.

Patrick Flanigan: Through the Eyes
of a Shut-Down Learner

I met Patrick on a photo shoot for the local newspaper when I was presenting to parents. Patrick started to talk to me about my work. He said that he struggled in school. As a result of our conversation, I sent Patrick a draft of *The Shut-Down Learner*. A week later, Patrick said reading it was a revelation to him. He was excited to talk about what the book meant to him. He related quite readily to the notion that as an adult he was able to be successful in pursuing a career in photography, whereas as a child and through high school, he did not feel successful at all. For much of his school career, Patrick was a shut-down learner.

How did Patrick find his way? What allowed him to become successful and not completely shut down and discouraged?

The following interview with Patrick is a wonderful example of the experience of a shut-down learner from the vantage point of a successful, productive adult. Patrick touches on the ingredients it takes to become successful.

RICHARD SELZNICK: Patrick, you said that reading this book was a revelation. How did it affect you?

PATRICK: I felt that way because I never did well in school. In your book, you mentioned third grade as the time that they start giving bigger reading assignments. That's when it started getting tough for me. The words were tough to decode, especially the bigger ones. I could remember very clearly in third grade looking at paragraphs of a story, trying to read them and forgetting what I read right away. I pretended to read. I was faking it. It was a horrible feeling. I hated all the worksheets. They were so tedious. I could totally relate to your description of the early school experience of the SDL. That was me.

From that time on, I never got great grades in school. I always got Cs and Ds. From high school I went straight to photography school, which is like a two-year vocational school.

I always knew I had certain talents and gifts, but up until I read your book, none of my feelings about school made sense to me. The revelation was that I felt validated reading your book. It validated my brand of thinking, which is something that never had happened before. My brand of thinking was always more visual and spatial. No one had ever said that to me.

It took this book to say, "This is what you are. You are intelligent, even gifted." I never could understand that about myself because of what happened to me in school. People just didn't realize it about me. They just saw the struggling kid, the one getting Cs and Ds. I felt dumb, and many people around me thought of me that way. Most people see a kid who's not amounting to anything. After all those years of seeing myself so negatively, reading this explanation was a revelation!

It was also a revelation that someone identified me, somebody understood me — my characteristics, my traits as a student, as a person growing up. Almost no one (including myself) understood that.

I could identify with everything, from hanging out a lot in the woods as a kid to everything else described. It was like an affirmation of everything I experienced.

RS: What do you remember about high school?

PATRICK: The thing about high school is that it's a social setting — girls and boys together. Some students did really well, you know, the college-prep track kids. Then there were the others. I was in that group — "the others." I was always in the remedial classes. It felt horrible. Just looking back on it, if I were educated a little differently like you suggest in the book, it could have been very different. If somebody taught me in a visual style, I would have done a lot better. I also needed to be encouraged more.

Thinking Macro to Micro

PATRICK: A lot of the techniques you use to help SDLs are methods I started to figure out on my own after photography school. For example, you talk about taking things in small parts. Once I was dating an architect and she showed me some of her plans from work. She explained about going from the "macro to the micro." You start with the big plan and then each little section will be the micro plan. I could visualize that better — macro to micro. It makes total sense to me. That's a template of knowledge for me, a way to approach things. I think training high-spatial kids in macro to micro thinking about all kinds of projects would help them a lot. They need to be trained to think this way. It would be something that they could relate to easily.

RS: So you keep thinking that way.

PATRICK: Right. I keep taking little pieces and think of them in the context of the larger picture and that's how I look at information. It would have been nice to learn it earlier, but much of it I had to discover on my own.

Visually Oriented Books

PATRICK: I found that books that were more visually oriented were easier for me to learn from. For example, I took a philosophy course in college and just the way the material was laid out on the page made it easier to comprehend. Some of the text was in little blocks and geometric shapes, such as sidebars, and when I'd study a chapter, I could digest these. It was like a visual landscape, and this format allowed me to process the information better. I'd go through a succession of the shapes in my mind one at a time and remember their location on the page. It was a great way for me to retain information. I would have never remembered the information if I just read it in straight text.

I always remember things in terms of a number or a picture. The number corresponds to a certain amount of information. For example, when I learned the different parts of a camera, I would go through the parts in linear fashion first and then assign each part a number. Each number was associated in my mind with a different part of the camera. I think it would be good to train people, especially visual types, to think like that.

So just to rephrase what I said about the revelation, it's the first time in my life that somebody understood where I was coming from. In your book you understood what was going on in my head, and this was tremendous.

RS: So it was a validation. My observation of SDLs is that they are discouraged, and they feel beaten down by all of these failed experiences.

PATRICK: Right, and then you have the social experiences that come of struggling in school and being seen as the slow child. All you see are the brainy kids, and at fifteen it's hard to get a perspective that says, "Well, they're smart for certain things and I'm smart for these other things." It's hard to get this perspective at that age—really at any age, for that matter.

Surviving High School

RS: How'd you stay afloat in high school? How did you not become a casualty?

PATRICK: I worked hard just to get by. My GPA was maybe a C average. There were other things that kept me going. I took on photography. I really got into photography when I was a freshman. That was one of the big things that kept me afloat. We didn't have photography class or anything in school, but I just started doing photography wherever I could. If there was a play, I did all the head shots. This meant a lot to me. I started to get people to see that I wasn't just this kid with nothing. It started to change how I saw myself, not a lot, but a little bit at a time.

Validation and Encouragement

RS: So you would get validation separate from academics?

PATRICK: Correct! Yeah, there were pats on the back like you talked about in the book. There was one teacher in particular. I remember doing her head shot for the play, and I remember her saying to me, "You know, you're really good at this; you could do this as a vocation." As soon as she said that, something clicked in my head. I felt, "You know, I think she's right." That one sentence stuck in my head. That was the one thing that mattered. Here was somebody seeing value in me. This had never really happened anywhere. It's exactly what you talk about — finding a way to encourage these kids. Help them see their value. Get them past their loser thinking. You were right — this is the answer.

RS: Isn't that amazing. You were so insecure in school, but someone you respected said, "You know, you're good at this," and it had tremendous impact. You could say that sentence of encouragement was life-changing.

PATRICK: Yeah, that was the one sentence that said, "You have talent," or "You are valuable" and it made all of the difference. It's amazing the impact that it had. Fortunately, she really encouraged me, and here I am at thirty-five making a good living in photography.

Impact of Relationship

RS: Were there other teachers along the way that encouraged you like that?

PATRICK: My parents were going through a messy divorce when I was in fifth grade, and there was a teacher who knew about all of the problems going on at home. He lived around the corner from me. He would invite me over to his house. He was married and had two kids, and I remember going over there and hanging out. We would do things like work on the computer and play chess, and we did other stuff that was educationally related.

RS: So, by taking you under his wing a bit, he really helped you?

PATRICK: Absolutely. My parents were going through such a nasty divorce, and everybody on the block knew about it. I really grew up feeling humiliated, and this one teacher who let me hang at his house made a big difference for me. *It really made me think that somebody cares and somebody thinks I'm a good guy.*

RS: It's interesting. It's almost like you're talking about layers of humiliation between the school and what was going on at home. It was like social and academic humiliation.

PATRICK: Yeah. I spent quite a bit of time having people reinforce that I was worthless. I went through a number of years of therapy to get perspective on it.

The Guy with the Camera

RS: How about sports in high school?

PATRICK: Nah, I wasn't a sports guy, but I was the guy with the camera.

RS: I think that would be good advice for the SDL, become the "guy or girl with the camera," or something similar.

PATRICK: Yeah, I often say that photography saved me from a lot of misfortune in my life. I'm also into filmmaking. I made short films that played in six festivals around the country and won international awards. I also write screen plays. When I was a kid I spent so much time in class daydreaming. Now, that is how I write screen plays. I can play whole scenes in my head. If I let my mind go, I can see the scenes happen. I think my daydreaming was very helpful.

It helped get me through school.

So I think the most important thing is to help mentor the kids and teach them how to value and use this visual-spatial talent that they have. That's what was so great in your book. That really struck a chord with me. It's like this gift that they don't understand.

PATRICK'S POINTERS

- Get kids past their "loser thinking."
- If you're a teacher, you can impact a kid tremendously. Patrick still remembers his high school teachers complimenting him on his photography. That changed his life.
- Recognizing the value in children could make all the difference in their future.

Patrick Flanigan can be reached by email at flaz2001@yahoo .com.

Rick Pullen: Shut-Down Learner and Father of an SDL

Mr. Rick Pullen is the Training Coordinator for the eastern region of the Laborers' International Union of North America. He is also the owner of his own consulting company. I met Mr. Pullen when he brought his son in for an evaluation.

RS: What are the different jobs that your union works with?

RP: I work for the laborers' union and with five other trades to construct buildings. We work with carpenters, electricians, plumbers, roofers, and ironworkers. We help them plan their jobs and move materials out. I also build bridges and work out in the field and out on the highway. When I came out to the field I was a superintendent running a $38 million road job. I had 140 employees working for me. I read plans and insurance and costing estimates. I did planning for the sets of crews and was involved with estimating materials and time.

RS: What percentage of the people that you interact with do you think fit the profile of an SDL?

RP: In my career, probably 75 to 80% of the people that I deal with fit the profile. They had difficulty with school and avoided going for a degree after high school. A large percentage of them would have struggled in school.

RS: You came to me as a parent concerned about your kid. How could this book potentially help other parents or adults who fit the shut-down learner profile?

RP: The number one thing that I think this book could help with is to relieve some of the stress between the parent and child. My parents knew I was intelligent, but they thought I was lazy. Just to break that negative interaction between a parent and child would be an amazing thing. For the parent to understand and relate to what their kid is going through would mean a lot. Since I went through it myself, it's very easy for me to relate to what my kid is going through now. Reading this book also helps me to relate to the people in my field better, particularly those that are involved in the training that I do.

RS: You previewed the manuscript of *The Shut-Down Learner* and my guess is that you could not help but reflect upon your own experience. What did you relate in terms of your background?

RP: What I related to mostly was that it defined the difficulties that I had through high school and the attitude that I had, because I thought I was an idiot—literally. I couldn't grasp some of the techniques in my math and science classes. It seemed to me that I had to work five times harder than everyone.

I didn't realize until I had gotten out of high school by the skin of my teeth and into the construction field that I had to make myself better as a teacher to relate to my students. I had to know students better and relate to their learning styles. So I started looking into what I was doing and got some schooling. I went to college and re-alized that I had a disability, because I had exactly what your book described. I was shut down at school. I had all the physical and mental capabilities. I could look at a project and dissect it and put it back together, but I couldn't explain how to do it and I certainly couldn't write about it. What I understood from your book was that there was a disconnect, something that wasn't working properly, even though I knew for that in so many areas I was very intelligent and well above average.

RS: Even though you seem like a very confident adult, would you say that school adversely affected your self-esteem? I would imagine that thinking you were stupid, you were very angry with yourself for many years.

RP: This was absolutely true. I was told by my high school guidance counselor that I would never amount to anything and I needed to get into the shop trades, because I was not college material. Later on in the course of going through the adult learning experience and teaching a variety of adults, I found out that my intelligence was well above average. I even took an IQ test to determine that I was very bright. It took many years for me to understand this though and the anger and hurt was very deep.

RS: When you were in high school, what would have been more helpful? What should a guidance counselor have told you?

RP: First off, you must be encouraging and not discouraging. I see this with so many of the adults that I deal with currently. I'm starting to do this with adults now, because I teach so many of the ones that you describe. Without a doubt, the best approach for this type of person is to get them out of the classroom and get them feeling successful. The classroom environment is a very close environment and is uncomfortable for a lot of people. If you tell me what you need done, then let's go out and do it. Let's get our hands on it and let's be part of it.

RS: We just finished a course this summer with your son to help him to think in more visual terms using concept mapping (see the section on Visual Leap in the appendix). How do you feel it went for him? It seems to me that it really tapped into his strengths as a spatial learner.

RP: As you know, my son is a very good reader, but he has tremendous difficulty expressing his thoughts in writing. I could give him a box of Legos and he can put together a complex design just by looking at the picture. He doesn't need the instructions and he would do it very quickly. It's easier for him to look at the picture than to read about what he is going to build. To tie in the reading and the writing with that ability as he did in the course this summer was just what he needed.

RS: Can you tell me more about the adult learners you work with?

RP: Many of them can get stuck in situations where they are miserable. You find people in careers that they hate. Their personal life turns miserable and much of it is rooted in their belief that they can't learn—that they're stupid. This belief is something they have been carrying around for a long time. If you give them the same kind of learning opportunities my son had this summer, I think it would give the adults the opportunity to say "Yes, I can learn this" and feel good about themselves.

I barely got through high school. Now I am working toward my master's degree in education. I overcame the emotional blocks by sheer will, by thinking, "There's got to be a way to learn this." When people think they can't learn, it's not a small impediment, it's a wall, and then the intense frustration mounts. If we can get out of traditional learning models for these people to a more hands-on approach, this would mean a lot. They have to start by understanding their own type of thinking.

RS: What are your hopes for your son?

RP: He loves anything to do with outer space. I could see him designing rocket ships and becoming involved with aeronautics. He would really do well with something like that because it excites him. I would also love for him to follow in my footsteps, because I can drive around in any one of six different states and point to things that I've constructed and that's an awesome thing. No two projects are the same, and it can be very exciting and interesting.

Helen, Mom of a Shut-Down Learner

Helen is the mother of a classic shut-down learner. I met her son Alex when he was twelve and in the sixth grade. At the time of this interview Alex was entering the eighth grade. Alex's school career has been an ongoing series of frustrations. The biggest hurdle is getting others to understand that Alex's issues are not purely motivational, as most teachers perceive him as someone who just doesn't try. Helen is a strong advocate for Alex. She works as a neurobiology professor at a university medical school. Alex's father is the owner of a landscaping company.

RS: So even when he was little, would Alex gravitate toward those activities that I describe in the book, such as building things with Legos and other hands-on play?

HELEN: He loved Legos. He could spend hours building, even at a young age. Even if he wasn't engaged in building activities, he still gravitated toward similar hands-on activities. Anything that involved manipulating, taking apart, and putting together he loved. He would enjoy doing those kinds of things all day.

Puncture Wound in the Tire

RS: The shut-down learner's motivation often seeps out, like the air seeps out of a pinhole in a tire, as they experience more and more failure. When do you remember the difficulty with school beginning to emerge for Alex?

HELEN: For Alex, it wasn't the air slowly seeping out. I think there was a big puncture in first grade because the teacher gave the kids worksheet after worksheet after worksheet. It was phonics. It was reading comprehension and addition. It didn't matter. It was entirely too much for him. He would come home at the end of the day with a half-dozen of these worksheets, which he was asked to complete for homework, on top of all the ones he did not complete in school. The teacher would send a note home saying, "This is what Alex did not do in class and he needs to complete them tonight." Can you imagine? First grade! He was six years old!

Well, if he didn't do it in class, he felt punished each evening. That was when the air gushed out. By the end of the year, we would just try to keep Alex's head above water by staying up-to-date with all those worksheets. He hated them. It was just a lot of busy work. Alex knew that by seven years old.

rs: Does the school understand his issues with reading fluency? It seems to me they always have a motivational explanation for Alex's issues — you know, "if he only tried harder."

helen: There's always been this question with Alex over the years — is it because he doesn't want to or he's having difficulty and he can't? The teachers always tell me that it's because he doesn't want to do the work. They have never, ever mentioned his reading fluency problems or the cognitive variability that you told us about. It's the same story every year. It's always described entirely as a motivational problem of his. He's telling us that he can't do it, or that he doesn't quite answer the questions. To us it's clearly a combination of the two — it's both motivation and legitimate difficulty with most of the tasks.

rs: What gets him excited in school, if anything?

helen: He's very good with hands-on stuff. He loves math and science. Those are the subjects that he views as his strengths. On the other hand, he will also get really excited about other subject matter when it's something that he can relate to like the catapult that he made.

rs: What do you think is missing for Alex in his educational experience?

helen: I would like for his teachers to find ways of tapping into Alex's curiosity. I would love to see Alex come home more enthusiastic and curious than he does now. I think if he were more fully engaged with hands-on activities like the building of the catapult for his Ancient Rome project, school would be a lot better for him. It's still too flat and one-dimensional for him too often.

RS: I discuss the relational aspects of school for the SDL in my book. Do you think that if Alex had somebody to take him around for a walk once in a while and show an interest in him, it would help him get his battery recharged emotionally?

HELEN: Yes, I think this would be tremendous. The math teacher has kind of done that. He's taken a real interest in Alex and some of the other kids who are having a little difficulty. They're probably all shut-down learners. They go to Mr. Brenner's room and they all hang out during lunchtime. It's great. They love it. They listen to CDs, and he cuts them some slack; it really makes a tremendous difference for them. It's like a refuge in their day.

Alex in High School

Alex is now in high school and I see him periodically to check in on him. By all reports, he is doing pretty well, but school continues to be an effort, especially the courses that involve a lot of reading and writing. Alex has connected very passionately to martial arts after school, and this is great for him. Keeping Alex afloat through high school will not be easy. Alex's parents very much want him to attend college. If Alex does go to college, he will need a great deal of support and guidance. So many SDLs get into college only to crash and burn after a semester or two. They have a great deal of difficulty with the lack of structure in the college environment. So many of the factors needed for success are not typically part of their repertoire. Planning, working toward a long-term goal, and staying on top of assignments are not a shut-down learner's best skills.

To help Alex with the rest of high school, he will need training with programs such as Visual Leap (www.thevisualleap.com). This will provide Alex with an approach perfectly suited to his strengths. Alex will learn planning and organizing using visual strategies and approaches, such as concept mapping, mind mapping, and webbing his thought process.

Alex also will be trained in assistive technology. The sooner Alex takes responsibility for his own learning through the use of technology, the better his experience will be. Alex needs to develop good habits with the technology. Programs such as Kurzweil 3000 and Dragon Naturally Speaking are good examples.

Finally, there will be the continual need to connect with Alex emotionally and to try to keep him from sabotaging himself. Alex has a quick temper and needs to learn coping skills, negotiating, and how to be flexible in his problem-solving process. These skills have not been easy to develop in Alex, but I have seen him make great strides and I am hopeful that he will continue to grow in his abilities.

Shut-Down Learner
Success Stories

I have met so many SDLs over the years. Some I have known from their teenage years, well into adulthood. Others I have met as adults, when they come in with their child for an evaluation. Similar themes run through their stories. Typically they do not look back at school fondly. School was their low point, a period of their life that they would rather forget. Into adulthood they were able to use their talents and abilities more successfully in ways that were not known in high school. Some made it through college and graduate school; others chose to develop their businesses and careers by bypassing school once they left high school. In the last chapter you heard the perspectives of two successful adults, Patrick Flanigan and Rick Pullen, who struggled as shut-down learners in school. In this chapter I briefly introduce you to other shut-down learners who have found careers that suit them.

Scott: Guitarist and Businessman

I met Scott when he was fifteen years old. I was a young psychologist. Scott was struggling in school, with very low motivation for academics. His parents were warm, supportive, and scared. They didn't like the direction that their shut-down learner was taking, which was clearly not down traditional academic paths.

However, Scott had a passion. He loved guitar, and he spent most of his waking hours practicing and studying the instrument. One of the best things for Scott was that he was mentored by a very accomplished musician. This musician guided Scott in how to become a successful independent adult in the field of music. Scott also received a great deal of counseling to help him gain perspective on who he was becoming.

The most important point to emphasize is that Scott was mentored by adults who saw qualities in him to develop. Mentoring is one of the most important gifts that can be given to a shut-down learner. Find someone who can guide him or her and let the SDL apprentice with the mentor. Someone has to take him under his wing to show that there is hope.

This mentoring relationship can be a formal one like Scott had with his teacher or it can be informal, like Patrick Flanigan had with his teacher.

Scott listened to the teachings that were given to him and his maturity and perspective grew over the years. As a young adult, Scott started to give guitar lessons to kids. One student led to another. Today Scott owns a thriving music teaching business, with more than ten employees under him. Scott plays in different clubs and has produced a number of his own CDs. He performs at many events, such as weddings and other life-cycle events.

Scott could never follow a traditional academic path. He muddled through high school and some college, but this type of schooling was not for him. Even though I didn't fully understand it at the time I counseled Scott, he was a classic SDL. He now is a fully independent, successful adult.

Yes, the SDL can get to the other side when given the right type of support and guidance. I am very proud to say that after twenty years, Scott and I are active friends, keeping close tabs on each other's lives and families.

Scott can be reached through his website, www.silvermusic studios.com.

FINDING MENTORS: HOW DID YOU BECOME A...?
- Kids need guidance, especially for fields that are not well-defined by their attending a professional school. Many people would be flattered to offer their expertise.
- Talk to people who may be willing to take your child under their wing.
- Post your interest in finding a mentor at the high school. People are often looking for ways to help kids.

Tim: The Chef

I met Tim when he was about fourteen. Tim was severely dyslexic and difficult. He hated school and was extremely challenging to his parents when it came to following the rules, succeeding with academics, and basically following the traditional program. Tim's father was a very successful businessman who overcame a severe learning disability.

I felt very close to Tim. He was a passionate kid, even though he was graying the hair of all the adults who dealt with him. Over the years, though, I lost touch with him.

Recently I got a call from Tim, now in his thirties. "Selznick," (none of my SDLs ever called me "Doctor") he said, "it's Tim." I knew who it was immediately.

He came to my office and we had a great conversation. One of the wonderful things that I learned about Tim was how successful he had become as a high-level chef. He was confident and capable, handling one of the most challenging of restaurants in a luxury hotel-casino.

The field of culinary arts is a classic example of an area in which many SDLs thrive. Such a field has all the right ingredients for success. It was so great to see how Tim turned out. School and managing the demands of the curriculum were so difficult for him that he could have easily become completely shut down and disconnected. By following his strengths, he got to the other side.

Tim followed the classic path of the shut-down learner. Once he survived the curriculum, he was able to follow his natural strengths.

Amy: Tough Teen, Creative Adult

Amy was possibly the toughest teen I worked with over the years. Oppositional, highly reactive, inflexible, and difficult are a few of the many negative attributes that come to mind when thinking about her. She came close to causing her family to separate as a result of the intensity of the battles waging over her. Amy also had significant reading, spelling, and writing problems.

Amy attended the Cooper Learning Center for learning therapy and visited me along with her parents for periodic counseling. The primary, often only, goal was to improve Amy's ability to communicate better with her parents. This goal was incredibly challenging.

Amy went to a private high school for children with learning problems and later attended a university arts school in the Philadelphia area. Specializing in graphic design, Amy started to receive praise from adults, something she had rarely heard over the years. Amy's sense of self started to turn around by degrees.

Amy is now in her late twenties, working for an advertising company. When she was in her teens I remember joking with her mother, "You'll see. You'll be having mother-daughter lunches when she's an adult. All of this will be a distant memory."

At the time that I said this it seemed like an impossible wish. I am happy to report that mother and daughter are lunching and fully enjoying each other's company. Amy is well on her way to becoming a productive, satisfied adult.

Alexander: Like Father, Like Son

Alexander is a very sweet eight-year-old. In third grade, he is finding that things are getting tough. Teachers see an inattentive child who has trouble staying on task. They are hinting (not so subtly) that he should be placed on medication. His parents are caring and concerned.

I was asked to evaluate Alexander, as his parents felt there was more going on with him than ADHD. They also were extremely reluctant to place Alexander on medication. The evaluation revealed the classic profile of the SDL — very weak language-based skills (semantic usage, processing sentences, verbal elaboration, etc.), with very solid abilities on spatial awareness and perceptual organization tasks. Alexander literally could have worked on the block patterns for hours with no sign of distractibility. Alexander always seemed to try very hard and he took great pride in each physical structure he created.

When I reviewed the findings with Alexander's parents, they were appreciative of having a broader understanding of their child. It was the first time that someone explained Alexander's issues beyond the explanation of ADHD and the need for medication. Most interesting was the father's responses. Our conversation went as follows:

FATHER: You know, I was exactly like him as a child.

RICHARD SELZNICK: Really. What do you remember?

FATHER: I struggled all the way through school. Now I'm the manager of a company that I took over from my father that sets up exhibit displays in conventions. I have great organizational skills. I can manage over fifty clients at a convention. Their exhibits are spread out over a large convention center. If someone called me while I was sitting here talking to you to ask me a question like where a piece was or how to find something needed for the job, I'd know exactly where to find it — sitting here!

This kind of ability was never, ever valued in school. I felt inadequate in school, yet I now can see how capable I am. I can do anything required for the job. I'm good at directing the support staff. I can see it all. I also find that I listen very closely to my clients. I don't just hear them and let the sound go in one ear and out the other. I listen. I have learned that listening is the key element in making a real difference. When I listen, I care. I empathize and I become pro-active and take action.

I know Alexander is just like me. I can see it in the way he plays. He can sit there for hours playing Legos and building, but reading and writing, forget about it. He can't last more than five minutes.

Alexander and his father are absolutely classic examples of SDLs. The hope is that by identifying Alexander early, a certain amount of heartache that the father experienced will be reduced for the son. Some of it they won't be able to avoid, but fully understanding the contributing variables to Alexander's school problems and finding him the right type of support changes the odds considerably for a positive outcome.

Josh: Severe Reading Disability/ Phenomenal Auto Mechanic

When Josh was seventeen he came to the Cooper Learning Center with one goal — to learn how to read well enough to take a course in auto mechanics.

His evaluation showed the typical SDL pattern, in the extreme. Josh quickly became a member of my SDL Hall of Fame. He scored in the 99th percentile for all of the spatial and perceptual tasks I gave him, yet only in the 10th percentile for verbal abilities. His reading skills clustered in the 5th percentile, with very severe decoding and reading fluency problems.

Josh was an extremely mature and motivated person. While he had shut down in earlier years of school, he now saw light at the end of the tunnel. He had been working part time in an auto repair shop and it became quickly apparent to the owner how gifted Josh was as a mechanic.

Auto mechanics has become quite sophisticated over the years with the increase in technology and there is reading involved, especially while attending the specialized trade schools that offer specific certifications.

Josh diligently came three times a week to be trained with the multisensory decoding methods used at the Cooper Learning Center. Josh took work home with him and practiced diligently with his parents. Josh also started the home-based reading fluency program. He was one of the more motivated students that we have seen at the center.

Josh worked on his reading skills for two intensive years and improved to the point where he was able to manage the auto mechanics course.

Today Josh is gainfully employed as an auto mechanic, and he loves his profession.

Kevin: Financial Analyst

Kevin loved thinking about business. He loved talking about stocks and the kind of business he wanted to pursue. He seemed to have a flair and confidence for the financial industry.

While not severely deficient in his reading skills, he had minor reading fluency problems and a relatively weak vocabulary. He never liked reading and avoided doing so whenever he could. He came to the Cooper Learning Center for some individual tutoring and counseling. He always enjoyed the counseling and was charming and easy to talk with on a range of topics.

Kevin had a phenomenal facility for seeing how things worked and his flair for mathematic reasoning was impressive. Middle school and high school were very challenging for him, though, and he gave his parents a very hard time.

He was able to get into college, attending a relatively noncompetitive school in the area and majoring in finance. In college he flourished, largely due to the fact that his strengths now matched the curriculum more closely.

He graduated college and sought a position in New York City. His first job allowed him to network (a clear skill of his) and quickly move up the ladder. Kevin is now thriving.

David: Dental School Student

When David was in high school, he was not easy to manage, and school represented a continual burden for him. He was fairly resistant to academics, and his parents wanted to evaluate him to find out whether there were any reasons for his resistance.

David had never had any previous assessments. A fun, gregarious kid in school, he was viewed by his teachers as an underachiever with an attitude. The testing was enlightening. Very solid with nonverbal and spatial tasks, David showed a good facility for mathematic reasoning. His reading, while not severely problematic by any standard, revealed subtle problems with reading fluency. He practiced reading fluency and received about a year of tutoring to help him decode complex words more effectively. He never liked reading, even after the tutoring, and avoided it at all costs.

David went off to college. I lost touch with him. After graduating, he contacted me for another evaluation as he was applying to dental school. He was hoping that he could get accommodations on the dental school entrance exam. This was ultimately given to him, as he continued to be a significantly slow reader. He did superbly on the portions of the test that assessed spatial thinking.

David is doing nicely in dental school. He feels that dentistry will be a career that will be perfectly suited for his personality and his strengths.

Alyssa: Physical Therapist

Alyssa was always very active and athletic. Some thought she was on the hyper side when she was in grade school. She played a variety of sports and excelled at them. She was almost always the leader of the team, and was seen as extremely popular and social.

Academics were another story. As confident as Alyssa was in the athletic and social arena, that's how insecure she was academically. She worked extremely slowly, which resulted in her assignments taking approximately double the normal amount of time to complete. She was overloaded by the tedium of worksheets, which were overused by her teachers. From Alyssa's point of view, school was an endless stream of worksheets, none of which motivated or interested her in the slightest.

She worked closely with one of the more motivating teachers at the Cooper Learning Center. This teacher reached her in ways that no one else seemed to be able to do in school. She started to feel more confident and her belief system began changing by degrees in a positive direction. Alyssa never became a strong student, but this change in her self-perception was able to get her through school.

She started attending a local community college while waitressing part time. Following community college she transferred to a local four-year college, showing a reasonable facility for sciences. She continued playing sports, and she became an assistant coach on a high school team. Some of the players were being treated by a physical therapist, and Alyssa targeted physical therapy as the perfect field for herself. Physical therapy was active and hands-on. She could never sit behind a desk in an office cubicle.

Alyssa started to become extremely motivated by the thought of becoming a physical therapist and she worked academically in ways that she never thought possible. She is now a physical therapist specializing in sports-based injuries, and she could not be happier.

Typical Shut-Down Learner Fields

These fields, jobs, and professions attract shut-down learners. To succeed in these endeavors, a person must be able to see how things

Independent business ownership
Architecture/design
Photography
Engineering
Accounting
Forensics
Sales
Advertising
Real estate development
    and sales
Information technology
Computers
Dentistry
Medicine (including
    related therapies such
    as occupational therapy,
    physical therapy)

Event planning
Film/digital video
Trade show design
Interior design
Landscaping
Graphic design
Auto industry
Trades (plumbing, carpentry,
    electrical, welding,
    sheet metal, etc.)
Culinary arts
Construction
Furniture design
Cabinet and furniture making
Apparel design
Fashion design
Jewelry/metal work

Typical Shut-Down Learner Fields, continued

Ceramics/Glass
Printmaking
Sculpture
Textile design
Digital media
Watch making
Illustration
Animation
Painting/drawing
Sculpture
Industrial design
Book arts

Music
Violin making and repair
Theater design and technology
Medical technician work
Acting
Set design
Film production
Video game design
Forestry and wildlife
House repair
Decorating
Cosmetic industry

work. Keep in mind that not everyone entering these fields or professions is a shut-down learner.

Conclusion

The premise of *The Shut-Down Learner* is that spatially-oriented kids have a unique set of strengths and weaknesses that does not lend itself well to success in school, as success is typically defined. Their strengths are not fully understood or valued. Their weaknesses are too apparent.

Cumulative layers of failed experiences result in the shut-down, disconnected posture seen in school and at home. School is not gratifying. Motivation seeps out like air slowly leaking out of a tire.

The most important way to overcome their status as a shut-down learner is to help them value and understand their strengths. Ideally, this should start at a young age, as the layers of negative, failed experiences will take their toll on the child's core sense of self. Certainly, in high school their unique talents and abilities surface, although they are not often recognized or channeled. Helping SDLs see these strengths can turn a life around. One encouraging sentence was all it took for Patrick Flanigan when he was in high school. One sentence cut through all of the negative beliefs.

In addition to recognizing and valuing shut-down learners for their unique strengths, finding a mentor to help guide students is the next most important consideration. Mentors can be teachers, counselors, plumbers, photographers — really anyone. You must find a way to get someone to take the shut-down learner under his wings for guidance and encouragement.

Shut-down learners are not a small segment of society. They come in all shapes and sizes. They can be found in a broad range of fields and jobs. Their negative experience in the early years could have been different. It is my hope that this book will help the shut-down learner see himself or herself in a more positive light.

APPENDIX
WINDS OF CHANGE:
INNOVATION AROUND THE COUNTRY

Many exciting, innovative programs, research studies, and educational experiences helpful to the SDL are taking place across the country. The following are noteworthy examples:

Logan Elementary School:
Putting Shut-Down Learner Principles to Work

Students at Logan Elementary School in Logan Township, New Jersey, are using a program called Flex Time to find a better way to learn. Developed by Principal Bob Fisicaro and implemented at the start of this school year, Flex Time is based on the ideas in *The Shut-Down Learner*. The program aims to let students explore their strengths instead of focus on taking tests.

"The educational system is primarily tailored to students with a verbal type of intelligence," Fisicaro said. "All students should learn how to read, write and reason, but our staff is honing in on educating the whole student."

In eight four-week sessions students can choose from classes in technology, puppetry, guitar, piano, perspective drawing and special math. In these 30-minute, small group classes they receive personal attention from teachers.

"Schools at the elementary level have become extremely academic and there's not much time for other types of intelligence to be recognized," said third grade teacher Teresa Ternyila. "This gives the students a chance to experiment with a creative curriculum and the kids really look forward to it."

To learn more about Flex Time, see www.logan.k12.nj.us.

KIPP: The Knowledge Is Power Program

KIPP, the Knowledge Is Power Program, is a national network of free, open-enrollment, college-preparatory public schools with a track record of preparing students in underserved communities for success in college and in life. KIPP began in 1994 when two young teachers—Mike Feinberg and Dave Levin—launched a program for fifth graders in a public school in inner-city Houston, Texas after completing their commitment to Teach For America. Today there are 99 KIPP schools in 20 states and the District of Columbia, serving more than 26,000 students in grades K-12.

Every day, KIPP students across the nation are proving that demographics do not define destiny. Over 90 percent of KIPP students are African American or Hispanic/Latino, and more than 80 percent of KIPP students are eligible for the federal free or reduced-price meals program. KIPP schools enroll all interested students, space permitting, regardless of prior academic record, conduct, or socioeconomic background.

KIPP schools emphasize high expectations in a supportive environment built on a partnership among parents, students, and teachers. By providing outstanding educators, longer school days, and a strong culture of achievement, KIPP is helping all students climb the mountain to and through college.

Nationally, more than 90 percent of KIPP middle school students have gone on to college-preparatory high schools, and over 85 percent of KIPP alumni have gone on to college.

In June 2010, Mathematica Policy Research, Inc. released the most comprehensive and rigorous report on KIPP schools to date. Researchers concluded that the vast majority of KIPP schools made significant and substantial gains in mathematics and reading, while serving a student population with lower entering test scores and a higher percentage of low income students than those of the neighboring public school districts.

To learn more about KIPP, go to www.kipp.org.

Jumpstart: An Innovative Preschool Program

There are signs very early that children may be struggling down the road with reading, spelling, and writing. Early identification and sensible, research supported programs can make can make a world of difference.

Jumpstart is an innovative program that was founded in 1993. Their website notes that, "Jumpstart is a leading nonprofit organization dedicated to ensuring that every child in America enters school prepared to succeed. To support this mission, we bring college students and community volunteers together with preschool children in low-income communities for a full school year of individualized mentoring and tutoring. Jumpstart's research-based curriculum is focused on building language, literacy, social, and emotional skills in preschool children, while providing our volunteers with a re-warding way to have lasting impact in their communities.

To cultivate a child's social, emotional, and intellectual readi-ness, Jumpstart brings college students and community volunteers together with preschool children for year long, individualized tu-toring and mentoring.

Since 1993, more than 70,000 preschool children across Ameri-ca have benefited from millions of hours of Jumpstart service. This year alone, Jumpstart volunteers are serving more than one million hours with 13,000 preschool children in more than 60 communi-ties across America.

To learn more about Jumpstart, go to www.readfortherecord.org.

Teach For America

Teach For America provides a critical source of well-trained teach-ers who are helping break the cycle of educational inequity. These teachers, called corps members, commit to teach for two years in one of 39 urban and rural regions across the country, going above and beyond traditional expectations to help their students achieve at high levels.

Teach For America's 20,000 alumni are playing critical leader-ship roles in the effort to improve the quality of public education in low-income communities. Armed with the experience, conviction, and insight that come from leading children to fulfill their poten-tial, Teach for America alumni are working from all sectors to shape schools, policies, and investments in low-income communities.

Teach For America corps members and alumni are leading some of the most successful efforts to close the achievement gap in com-munities nationwide.

To learn more about Teach For America, go to: www.teachfor america.org.

Learning to Think Spatially:
The National Academy of Sciences Report

The National Academy of Sciences presented the findings of a committee investigating spatial thinking as it applies to schools and society. This overview, GIS (Geographic Information Science) as a Support System in the K-12 Curriculum, provides a technical analysis and overview of spatial thinking (www.nap.edu/catalog/11019.html).

In this report, specific recommendations for schools emphasize the importance of understanding spatial thinking and ways that it can be developed, nurtured, and encouraged.

The report is well worth reading for any educator interested in a state-of-the-art overview of the scientific aspects of this topic. It also would be good for parents who want to pass the concepts on to teachers.

This statement from the report highlights the importance of understanding spatial thinking: "Spatial thinking is currently not systematically instructed in the K-12 curriculum despite its fundamental importance and despite its significant role in the sets of national standards for science, mathematics, geography, etc. . . . There is a major blind spot in the American educational system."

Temple University's Spatial Intelligence
and Learning Center

As a graduate of Temple University's Graduate School of Education, I was excited to learn about Temple establishing a Spatial Intelligence and Learning Center. This center was established with a $3.5 million grant from the National Science Foundation. Along with Temple, there are SILC centers at the University of Washington, Carnegie-Mellon University, Boston University, University of California-San Diego, and Gallaudet University.

Temple's 2007 winter newsletter states, "The center's goal is to understand spatial learning and to use this knowledge to develop programs and technologies that will transform educational practice and support the capability of all children and adolescents to develop the skills required to compete in a global economy."

The quote that really caught my eye was the statement from the director of the center, Dr. Nora Newcombe: "We believe that there's an important type of learning — spatial learning — that's being neglected. We pay a lot of attention to teaching reading and mathematics, but spatial learning is really important in mathematics, science, and engineering, especially in technological disciplines."

Most SDLs would agree with this statement wholeheartedly. If spatial learning had been more formally a part of their school experience, they would have escaped much of their anguish.

To learn more about the work of the centers, see www.spatial learning.org.

The Cooper Learning Center, Department of Pediatrics, Cooper University Hospital

Cooper University Hospital is the largest teaching hospital in the South Jersey region. The Cooper Learning Center, a division of the Department of Pediatrics, has worked with thousands of children since 1995.

As director of the Cooper Learning Center, I am very proud of the effectiveness of our program. Specialized tutoring ("learning therapy") focuses on developing core decoding, reading comprehension, and written output problems. To the extent possible, experts offering assessments strive to be non-labeling, preferring to view the child and his myriad of strengths along with the areas of need.

Recognizing that many children who need these services cannot afford them, the Cooper Learning Center also has offered scholarships, making the services low cost or totally free to children from lower socioeconomic backgrounds. For example, generous corporate donations from the Jeff & Tracy Brown Foundation and Anne Koons of Prudential Realtors have enabled a thriving summer reading program to early-grade children in a neighboring school in Camden.

The Cooper Learning Center also has developed active partnerships with different schools in the region. This combination of a larger hospital system working closely with neighborhood schools and partnering with business in the community is the ideal for the future. Schools cannot do it alone, nor can parents. The work is too involved and the issues too complex.

So many children coming through the center over the years are shut-down learners. While the center cannot claim to have succeeded with every one, the mission remains the same — to value each child as unique and to help them to the extent possible with their skills and their understanding of themselves.

For more information on the center, see www.cooperlearning center.org.

Cooper Learning Center
4011 Main Street
Voorhees, NJ 08043
856-673-4900

"Experimental School Flourishes in Camden, New Jersey"

This was the headline from a story by Matt Katz in the *Courier Post*, a South Jersey newspaper. The school, MetEast, is one of 40 Big Picture Schools in the country. The principal of the school states in the article that "MetEast kids learn the same skills as children in other schools, we're just delivering the information in a different context."

What makes this school different? The article offered these points:

Two-year-old MetEast High School is a public school that uses a model created by Rhode Island-based Big Picture Learning, a forty-school national network backed by the Bill and Melinda Gates Foundation.

Students attend internships on Tuesdays and Thursdays and spend at least two hours each day in small classes with teachers or advisers. Beyond that, students work with their parents and advisers to create their own curriculum that encompasses all the basic subjects.

Advisers visit students' homes, meet with them one-on-one each week to talk, and remain their teacher through all four years.

Instead of tests, students make exhibitions four times a year showing the work they've done. Students also write essays charting their progress.

The school is adding a grade each year. In September, there will be ninety-three students, from ninth to eleventh grade.

SDLs desperately need to experience a sense of connection in school. MetEast and Big Picture Learning go a long way toward providing such a connection.

Big Picture Learning

Big Picture Learning, formerly The Big Picture Company, was founded by educators Dennis Littky and Elliot Washor. In 1995, they began collaborating with Rhode Island policymakers to design a student-centered high school, and created the Big Picture Company, a non-profit organization devoted to national education reform as a launching pad for what has now become a national education reform movement. Here is their mission statement:

> Big Picture Learning is a nonprofit organization that believes schools must be personalized, relevant to the students, and connected to the real world. Big Picture Learning schools educate one student at a time within a community of learners. We help young people, including underserved urban students, become lifelong learners, productive workers, and engaged human beings. The school design is built on three basic principles: 1) learning must be based on the interests and goals of each student; 2) curriculum must be relevant to people and places in the real world; 3) students' abilities must be measured by the quality of their work. We believe that the education system must ensure that students and families are active participants in the design and authentic assessment of each child's learning. Schools must be small enough to encourage the development of a community of learners, and to allow for each child to be known well by at least one adult. School staff and leaders must be visionaries and life-long learners. Schools must connect students, and the school, to the community—both by sending students out to learn from mentors in the real world and by allowing the school itself to serve as an asset to the local

community and its needs. Finally, schools must allow for admission to, and success in, college to be a reality for every student, and work closely with students, families, and colleges throughout — and beyond — the application process.

In addition to designing and supporting Big Picture Learning schools with this philosophy, Big Picture Learning continually innovates and tests tools and techniques to make our schools better. We will continue to refine components of our schools. Every lesson learned through our research and practice will give us added leverage to influence public policy.

Wow! It sounds like shut-down learner heaven. Note the emphasis on relationship and mentoring in the mission statement. This is exactly what the SDL needs to overcome the layers of defeat and negativity.

For more information, see www.bigpicture.org.

The North Bennet Street School in Boston

Many people just out of high school do not know where to turn. The North Bennet Street School is a place for those with SDL profiles to consider. The following is taken from www.nbss.org:

The North Bennet Street School has been training people for employment since 1885. It pioneered the concept of intensive instruction in a classroom/shop setting for the sole purpose of learning a trade. All of our courses prepare graduates for work in fields that require craftsmanship: skillful use of hand tools and power equipment; informed choice of appropriate materials; knowledgeable and creative problem-solving grounded in awareness of the best solutions of the craft over many years; and a commitment to the highest quality of work.

North Bennet Street School has a distinct reputation for excellence. It is more than a school where students learn the comprehensive elements of their chosen field; it is a place that sustains tradition in craftsmanship. Students come to North Bennet Street School from all corners of the globe to enroll in our programs. As diverse as the offerings are, they are tied together by the simple fact that in each program, students learn the time-honored skills and methods that produce work of the highest standards.

North Bennet Street School remains committed to the best part of the apprenticeship system of learning. Practical projects are the main substance of students' training. Beginning with the first assignment and continuing through the course, a student takes on increasingly difficult work. This method develops not only hand skills but also an understanding of procedures used in the trade. Each project builds on previous learning and requires the student to solve more complex problems. There are lectures and suggested reading material, but the practical application of these lessons at the bench is the most important element. While working at the bench, advice and information is conveyed in a practical context at the time when a student needs it. Lessons learned this way are not easily forgotten.

The design of courses and their content has been developed with the help of employers and trades people in each field. They have made sure that course content is thorough. The instructors are responsible for guiding students through the course so that they will be ready to go to work after graduation. They expect not only that students perform required work, but also that they do it well. This means continued practice through the course.

The North Bennet Street School
39 North Bennet Street
Boston, MA 02113
617-227-0155
www.nbss.org

Visual Leap

Over lunch, Jesse Berg, owner of Visual Leap, passionately explains his view of different learning paths:

> When it comes to school and learning, some people are born with a mind like a Honda Accord and learning is like driving down a highway. It is a pretty smooth process, and the role of school is to even out the bumps in the road. Other people are born with a mind like a Jeep 4x4. For them, learning is like driving in the wilderness, with limitless possibilities, but no trails to follow. These creative people require unique strategies to navigate their mental terrain and organize their ideas. School doesn't do that much for these folks. However, when they are taught learning strategies that match how they think, these learners can see possibilities and opportunities that are not visible from the road.

SDLs are definitely in the off-road category.

On a mission to train people to think in visual terms, Berg feels that mind mapping is a skill that can help everyone to organize their thinking and to be more productive—even the highly gifted.

Said Berg, "My childhood friend is one of the smartest people I know. He's a professor at a major university. I trained him to diagram his ideas and now he uses this technique all the time. These methods are useful for all kinds of learners and can help untangle the most complicated ideas."

While visual methods are universally useful, Berg has found them uniquely effective for SDLs because they help these learners to harness their creativity, organize their ideas, and navigate their own "off-road" style of learning.

Visual thinking, also called visual learning, is a proven method in which ideas, concepts, data, and other information are associated with images and represented graphically. Webs, concept maps, idea maps, and plots, such as stack plots and Venn plots, are some of the techniques used in visual learning to enhance thinking and learning skills.

Visual thinking is intuitive and easy to learn. It can unlock one's academic potential. Visual Leap programs use visual thinking software as a learning tool, and this software accelerates the learning process.

For more information, see www.thevisualleap.com.

Tiger Woods Learning Center

The Tiger Woods Learning Center opened in 2006 as one of the philanthropic missions of the Tiger Woods Foundation (www.twfound .org). The website's description of the program is as follows:

> The Tiger Woods Learning Center opened its doors to Southern California students in early January, providing interactive enrichment programs to promote career exploration and preparation in areas such as forensic science, engineering, aerospace, video production, and home design. The TWLC is a 35,000-square-foot, 14-acre education facility built to take young people beyond their

normal classroom experience through a unique afterschool curriculum rooted in science, math, and language arts. The mission is to provide young people with a broader perspective of the world; a clearer understanding of his or her own skills; and the tools to achieve long-term personal success.

To accomplish this, the TWLC employs the most advanced technology and educational tools along with caring teachers and dedicated mentors. The TWLC features seven classrooms, a computer lab, a multimedia center, student lounge, 200-seat auditorium, and café.

Almost all the SDLs I know would love a program such as the one offered at the TWLC.

For more information on the Tiger Woods Learning Center, see www.twlc.org.

GarageBand in the Curriculum: The Newgrange School

Music and computers are fundamental to most teenagers. These are an especially big part of the landscape of the SDL and are areas where these kids can really excel. Music loads on a variety of different abilities. Some of the more involved abilities include spatial organization skills. Musicians can see patterns and relationships. Spatial thinkers tend to be oriented toward endeavors such as playing music. This skill comes to them fairly naturally.

GarageBand is a recording-studio software program from Apple Computers. The software enables students to engage in sophisticated music composition without having to use standard musical notation. Kids create music directly on the computer.

The Newgrange School in Hamilton, New Jersey (www.the-newgrange.org), specializes in teaching children with learning and reading disabilities and has implemented a GarageBand elective as part of its curriculum. Students in grades three through twelve are able to enroll in a GarageBand class that meets two to four times a week.

As reported in a newsletter published from the school, the kids are extremely motivated by this addition to the curriculum. This program provides for an array of hands-on activities in music composition and production, keeping the kids connected in ways that the standard curriculum does not. They get their emotional and motivational battery recharged by spending time in such classes. School no longer seems like an endless challenge for them.

Hands-On Science: Possibilities in the Classroom

Earlier I talked about Brian, one of my favorite SDL kids. If you recall, Brian spent a great deal of time at home with his elaborate terrariums, primarily assembled from local pond life. Even though it's been a long time since I saw Brian, I can well remember him talking about how bored he was in school, even biology class. The basic fact was Brian needed more of a hands-on experience than what was being provided in the school. Textbooks and worksheets were not capturing his imagination. They were having the opposite effect.

A recent article in *Education Week* (April 16, 2008) discussed Michael Nagle's elementary class school in Cambridge, Massachusetts.

As Nagle noted in the article, "The most exciting [and educational] experiences have always been when kids make their own inventions."

Along with teaching hands-on science to elementary school age kids, Nagle is the director of Camp Kaleidoscope — a hands-on science and art camp in Cambridge.

As stated on the website for Camp Kaleidoscope (www.camp-kaleidoscope.org), Nagle has been teaching hands-on math and science for the past three years to elementary-aged kids in a variety of settings (afterschool programs, homeschooling groups, and of course, at Camp Kaleidoscope.) He founded Camp Kaleidoscope in 2006 and graduated from MIT with a math degree in 2005. His other teaching adventures have included volunteer teaching SAT prep to inner-city youth in Boston, teaching intro chemistry and calculus at MIT, and teaching a free Advanced Placement calculus course for high schoolers. His latest project is starting a hands-on, noncoercive elementary school that was slated to open in September 2008.

So many of the SDL kids that I have known, such as Brian, need this type of experience. Frankly, all kids would benefit from this type of learning. It's just that the SDL kids need this very badly.

To learn more about the wonderful programs offered at Camp Kaleidoscope, email or call kaleidoscope@mit.edu, 617-895-7676.

America's Promise Alliance: Every 26 Seconds Another Child Drops Out

There is a crisis in the country that is becoming greater every day. According to The America's Promise Alliance (www.americaspromise.org), every twenty-six seconds another child drops out of school. The percentage of these children coming from urban African-American and Latino communities is alarmingly high.

How many of these children would fit the characteristics of the shut-down learner profile? There is no easy way to know, but my guess would be quite a lot.

The America's Promise Alliance is a network of prominent civic and educational leaders looking to stem the tide of the dropout rate in the country. The alliance is built around "Five Promises," which are:

- Caring adults
- Safe places
- A healthy start
- Effective education
- Opportunities to help others

See www.americaspromise.org.

RAPSA: Reaching At-Promise Students Association

The Reaching At-Promise Students Association is a nonprofit organization whose mission is to be a resource for teachers, parents, and community members who work with struggling learners. RAPSA believes that all students have the right to achieve at their greatest potential to become educated and employable members of the community.

RAPSA provides professional development and practical teaching strategies that address the needs of students for whom traditional educational methods have failed. Through workshops, trainings, and conferences, RAPSA shares innovative, standards-aligned assignments and methodologies for immediate classroom use. RAPSA promotes the capabilities and accomplishments of at-promise students by working in collaboration with local businesses and developing valuable networking opportunities.

RAPSA is an enthusiastic and dedicated organization committed to meeting the needs of a diverse at-promise (also known as "at-risk") student clientele population.

Check out www.rapsa.org, www.atpromiseconference.org, and www.leaders.rapsa.org.

RAPSA
2605 Temple Heights Drive, Suite F
Oceanside, CA 92056
800-871-7482

Bill and Melinda Gates Foundation

As part of its philanthropic mission, the Bill and Melinda Gates Foundation focuses on a variety of issues regarding education. The foundation's website (www.gatesfoundation.org/education) features many articles that are relevant to the SDL.

Books

There are a number of books on topics related to the ones in *The Shut-Down Learner:*

Multiple Intelligences: The Theory in Practice, A Reader by Howard Gardner (ISBN: 0-465-01822-x)
Upside-Down Brilliance: The Visual-Spatial Learner by Linda Kreger Silverman, Ph.D., (ISBN: 1-932186-00-X)
Raising Topsy-Turvy Kids: Successfully Parenting Your Visual-Spatial Child by Alexandria Shires Golon (ISBN: 1-932186-08-5)

If You Could See the Way I Think: A Handbook for Visual-Spatial Kids by Alexandria Shires Golon (ISBN: 1-932186-09-3)

Right-Brained Children in a Left-Brained World: Unlocking the Potential of Your ADD Child by Jeffrey Freed and Laurie Parsons (ISBN: 0-684-84793-0)

Late, Lost, and Unprepared: A Parent's Guide to Helping Children With Executive Functioning by Joyce Cooper-Kahn & Laurie Dietzel (ISBN: 978-1-890627-84-3)

Visual-Spatial Learners by Alexandra Shires Golon (ISBN: 10: 1-59363-324-6)

These are some good vocabulary books to use with shut-down learners:

504 Absolutely Essential Words (5th Ed), 2005, Bromberg, Murray, Liebb, Julius & Traiger, Arthur. Barrons, Hauppage, NY. (ISBN: 0-764-2815-9)

1100 Words You Need to Know, 2000, Bromberg, Murray & Gordon, Melvin. Barrons, Hauppage, NY. (ISBN: 978-0-7641-1365-9

Websites

Here are some websites that cover topics discussed in this book:

www.ldonline.org — A great resource for a variety of issues related to learning disabilities

www.interdys.org — The International Dyslexia Association

www.schwablearning.org — Highlighting the Great Schools Foundation and the Professor Garfield Foundation

www.allkindsofminds.org — A wealth of information on struggling learners
www.chadd.org — The nation's leading nonprofit organization
   serving individuals with ADHD and their families
www.ldanatl.org — The Learning Disabilities Association of
   America
www.wilsonlanguage.com – Wilson Language Training is dedicated to providing the teaching community with the resources
   needed to help their students become fluent, independent
   readers.

These sites offer great resources and a variety of information on
visual spatial learning:

   www.gifteddevelopment.com
   www.visual-learners.com
   www.visualspatial.org
   www.giftedservices.com
   www.thevisualleap.com

PERMISSIONS

What to Do with the Shut-Down Learner

Type II Reading Remediation. Excerpted with permission from *7 Keys to Comprehension: How to Help Your Kids Read It and Get It!* by Susan Zimmermann and Chryse Hutchins, Three Rivers Press, New York, 2003.

ABOUT THE AUTHOR

Dr. Selznick is a psychologist, a nationally certified school psychologist, and a graduate school professor. As the Director of the Cooper Learning Center at Cooper University Hospital, Dr. Selznick oversees a program that assesses and treats a broad range of learning and behavioral problems in children. The Cooper Learning Center is the leading program in its region, offering not only assistance with children, but also parent and teacher training programs.

In addition to his role as the Director of the Cooper Learning Center, Dr. Selznick functions as a school consultant, and throughout the year he speaks to numerous parent groups, schools, and regional conferences on topics such as dyslexia, parenting, bullying, and ADHD. He has been a guest on radio talk shows throughout the region.

Dr. Selznick strives to offer his audiences and patients with practical and applicable strategies for the challenging issues they face. He hopes to provide parents and teachers with the necessary methods to help children with academic problems. A native of Staten Island, New York, Dr. Selznick currently lives in Haddonfield, New Jersey, with his wife, Gail, and two children, Julia and Daniel.

To contact Dr. Richard Selznick and to learn about a growing community of shut-down learners and mentors, please see www.shutdownlearner.com.